Bipolar Blues

Carol Neves

DEDICATION

In Memory of Danna..

CONTENTS

1 MOLLY'S STORY

Is there a word for running naked through the streets or for the torment of thoughts racing faster than one can speak them? Is there a word for sleepless nights or spending money like water running through your fingers? Is there a way to define following every whim that presents itself and ending up without a home? Is there an explanation for disregarding and abandoning your children or dragging them along to witness the drama of your sexual exploits? Is there any way to understand the painful reality of a brain gone awry and buzzing like a mad bumblebee?

Bipolar Disorder is defined as a major mental disorder of mood with swings from mania to depression. In the manic phase, my father experienced racing thoughts and surges of energy. Hyperactivity does not begin to describe Dad as he flitted from one activity to another. He sought social activity like a moth drawn to a flame. His mania was extremely hot and fiery. His need for sleep diminished and his sexuality heightened. Ideas burst into his consciousness. His speech was pressured and rapid as his thoughts moved quickly from one topic to another. He brimmed with physical and mental energy. He made reckless decisions, committed sexual indiscretions and teetered on the border of financial ruin. After the manic energy was spent, Dad plummeted into the depths of depression. His mind slowed down to such a degree that any decision seemed almost impossible for him to make. He experienced insomnia and sleep disturbances, such as difficulty getting to sleep, troubled sleep with frequent waking or early morning awakening with inability to return to sleep again. He lost his appetite and his weight dropped. He had energy loss, feelings of lethargy, inertia, slowed speech and movement. In addition to depressed mood, lack of energy and sleep disturbances, Dad complained of headaches, backaches and stomach problems.

The hallmarks of Dad's ascent into mania were his late night arrivals at home, drinking, filling the house with friends and talking non-stop. He spent money as if it grew on trees. He arrived at home with new cars, new boats, new clothes, new friends, new pets and new projects. No one existed in his realm except himself as he scurried about chasing the brightness that had eluded him while depressed. As his mania ebbed, he gradually slowed down like a wind-up toy until he sat frozen in his chair in front of the television in silence. He enjoyed nothing. He was exhausted, drained of the percolating energy that had driven him. Now he talked to no one. Everything that had fascinated him and everything that he had purchased disappeared from view. Nothing remained. Nothing mattered. The fire had gone out.

Dad's brilliance, knowledge, fortitude and compassion helped sustain him in his practice as a physician. His career was peppered by psychiatric hospitalizations to stabilize his mood on medication in order to return him home and to work. Over time, Dad became dependent on alcohol and addictive prescription medications. His dependence grew like an over-watered melon. His mind was dancing to his prescribed psychotropic medications, Jim Beam and his self-prescribed barbiturates. Falling down stairs, crashing his car and running naked through the streets became regular events in Dad's life.

Born and named Molly Ann Edwards, the first child and only daughter of Daniel and Regina Edwards, I came into the world during my father's residency. I was born under a bad sign. My mother told me repeatedly the story of the day I was born. My father viewed my tiny body, walked into the street in front of the hospital and was hit by a bus. We shared the same hospital roof on my birthday. Dad, Mom and I rolled out of the hospital. Dad recovered and walked back to his doctor job a few months later. My brother, Oliver, was born a few years later without major incident. My family lived near Boston in a big old house on a corner, on the top of a gently sloping hill. Grass surrounded the house, four rooms on the first floor, three rooms on the second floor, providing ample space for family drama.

Big houses stand like elephants in the mist. I hate getting out of bed in the morning. I hate breakfast. No moments of joy in the morning come after age five. School shatters my budding life. I am dragged kicking but not screaming, just gently weeping into a huge, smelly room and left with thirty strangers. I go to my first day of school. Isolation, boredom and fear haunt my every school day. By second grade, I know the inevitability of having to attend school. I accept the boredom, the confinement and overcome my fear by excelling at schoolwork.

Our family rotated around Dad like a merry-go-round. Mom, my brother Oliver and I reflected Dad's mood like planets around the sun. If Dad was manic, we were bouncy. If Dad was depressed, we were quiet and motionless. When manic, Dad puked every morning from his late nights of drinking and carousing. Nobody mentioned the retching sounds he made as if vomiting and dry heaving were a normal part of Dad's morning preparations to get ready to go to work. His manic energy drove him to seek pleasure and stimulation. His depressed mood sapped his energy. When manic, his attention rapidly shifted from one thought to another with lightening speed, attending to outward stimuli; when depressed he appeared lost within himself, attending only to his inner reality.

Dad is manic, driving his car fast, too fast. I sink down in the passenger seat. Oliver squirms in the back seat. I'm scared, silent, shaking. My feelings rush over me like ice water. I pretend I'm invisible. I am disappearing slowly. Dad is depressed, moving around the house like a slug. He sends out darts of irritability we try to dodge. Living with Dad is like living on a minefield. I work on perfecting my invisibility. I live in a topsy-turvy world with nothing to grasp for safety. I am powerless as my father zooms into mania or plunges into despair. The bipolar years swirl inside me, around me and in my dreams. My father's blood flows through my veins causing mania, bursts of creativity, hypersensitivity, sleepless nights, depression and debilitating insecurity. My father's legacy provides the mountains and valleys of my life. My topography has lower peaks and higher valleys than Dad's. The weather patterns are replicated in my DNA. Dad and I may appear as different as night and day but I have learned Dad's moods and carry Dad's genes. Is there any hope for me?

The bipolar years seemed endless. Anything could and did happen. Dad had periods of calm and normal moods, creating a hiatus between his mania and his depression. With each episode of mania and depression, he was worse, more severe. He was hospitalized frequently and put on medication after medication. His treatment was helpful for periods of time but nothing seemed to prevent his decline into madness.

Dad is home from the hospital. Antidepressants have lifted his mood and erased his symptoms of depression, fatigue, insomnia, irritability, headaches and stomach pains and most importantly his suicidal thoughts. He's back in the family and back at work. Mom files away the trauma of finding her husband hanging in the closet with a blue tinge to his face. She is the queen of denial, going to extraordinary lengths to keep her feelings at bay. Hope and denial entwine Dad and Mom in the delusion of Dad's having been cured following his 'episodes'.

Dad had a reputation as an excellent doctor. Knowledge of his manic misbehavior was limited to law enforcement and a small subset of hospital staff. When manic, his intense sociability extended to those with whom he worked as he invited them to join in his big parties. Dad had two faces, the respected doctor and the crazy man. When Dad was well, he was normal. When he was crazy, he was abnormal. He performed his medical duties well until mania or depression struck hard like a hammer and the police were called to attend to his car accidents or to pull him off the streets when he was out of control. The hospital staff was aware of Dad's late night parties and sexualized behavior but no one talked of Dad's indiscretions. They were bound by a code of silence to protect his professional reputation.

I played my family like a computer game, attempting to make each member contribute just enough to make a functional family but it was too exhausting for me. When the wild bipolar card was added to the structure, the house of cards crashed down, scattering in all directions. Mom pulled up beside the wreck and pointed Oliver and me in the right direction but we were too preoccupied with fear and doubt to duck and cover. No one was home to soothe our feelings or to answer our questions.

My emotional makeup was hardwired into my brain in the stressful climate of my Dad's mood swings. Tossed and turned by Dad's bipolar breezes and storms, I drifted away, retreating to a dark place, eventually starting my own bipolar history. Having adapted to a crazy home life, my thinking, feelings and behavior became abnormal. My disappearing act became perfected. "Molly, what's up with you?" was a question my mother always asked me as she spun in her land of denial and duty. I hid in my bedroom closet under my clothes eating potato chips from a big bag. Salt, sweat and tears blended in my mouth like ocean water clogging my throat causing me to choke my way back.

My depression started like a bad case of the flu. I tried to toss my depressed thoughts out like dirty dishwater but soon my dark thoughts became a major motion picture, starring me as the most worthless girl ever born. Suicidal thoughts took control of my mind like a tune that would not quit. I became alarmed as I thought of ways to end my life in visions of drowning, cutting myself or jumping off a cliff. I was frightened. I got into bed under the covers, curled up in a ball and cried myself into a stupefied, exhausted state until I was numb.

Turning seventeen clicked my clock and sent me spiraling down into my first big bad depressed mood as my high school graduation approached. In early spring, feelings of hopelessness and despair fell upon me like a black cloud with anxiety gnawing at me like a big rat. I could not bear to be around anyone. I hid out in my bedroom or in the darkened living room at night while the rest of the family watched TV in the family room. I lay on the sofa in the dark, staring out the window at the street light. Thoughts of death wafted through my mind with the belief that I would die imminently.

As my energy level decreased, I headed for the sofa or my bed as soon as I returned home from school. At school, I mustered enough energy and attention to make it through my classes. My friends were twittering with talk of boys, graduation and summer plans. They barely noticed my retreat. Dad emerged briefly from his manic whirlwind and noticed my depressive behavior. Dad scored high in attunement as he recognized my distress but he failed to help me as he was being swept along by a current too strong to resist. Mom noticed me a few days before graduation. I was completely unprepared for graduation. I was shocked to realize I was still alive. Part of me was dead. I perceived the world around me as through cotton batting. I no longer enjoyed playing or listening to music. I enjoyed nothing. Spring normally excited and enlivened me but this spring of my last year of high school found me consumed completely by depression. My lack of response made me even heavier at heart. I felt as if I had lost a close friend.

"Who was that happier person? What has happened to me? What the hell will I wear to graduation and what the hell will I do about the senior prom?"

Mom searched the house and found me lying on my bed in my pajamas in the middle of the day, staring at the ceiling. She asked, "Molly, are you ready for graduation? Did you go shopping with your friends and get a dress?"

"I don't have a dress."

"Are you feeling well? Are you feeling sick? Do you have your period?"

"I'm fine. No period."

"Well, let's go get you a dress to wear to graduation!"

We drove in silence to the mall. I felt strange as if I had left my body, drifting along the highway to the mall with my mother at the wheel of the car. I could see the grass, the trees, the houses, the other cars moving as if in a dream but I was awake. My thoughts focused on the strange emptiness within. I was having a strange new experience of life. I expected to die and I could not envision a future. A slow sense of relief spread through me as I realized death would bring an end to my suffering but panic quickly ensued as I realized I might die. I was afraid to die. I wanted to die but I was afraid to die.

At the mall, I modeled dresses until my mother selected one for me. My thoughts revolved around a biting sense of guilt. I could not deduce my crime but I was convinced beyond doubt that I was guilty and deserved to die. Mom paid for the dress. My life was going on without me. I numbly followed my mother around the mall. She carried on a one-sided conversation with me not noticing my lack of response as she picked out appropriate items for my big day. Her voice penetrated my consciousness but her statements were without meaning to me. I attended solely to staying near her as I was overwhelmed by the mall frenzy. Cold and sweaty, I feared being separated from my mother. If I lost her, I would drop down on the floor and be trampled by the mall people. Exhaustion wracked me as if I had never slept in my entire life. I envisioned my bed at home across a desert like a mirage.

Finally at home, Mom directed me to model my new dress for my father and my brother. I followed her instructions, put on the dress and swirled around a few times to their compliments. In my room, I tossed the dress on a chair and sank onto my bed. I knew I'd have to drag myself to dinner. I worked hard to keep my parents from knowing how far away I had traveled from them. My father had read the clues but in his manic whirl could not stop long enough to attend to my sinking status. We occupied opposite ends of the mood scale on a skewed see-saw. My mother and brother resided in the middle of the fulcrum holding an illusion of our family together. Mom tried to rein my father in from his indiscretions and to push me into action with my life. She managed to patch things at a superficial level but my father's ascent could only be stopped with the right combo of meds and my descent would follow its course as water finds its lowest level.

I went to the prom with a boy whom I had known since elementary school. When we compared notes about the prom and discovered neither of us had plans to go, we decided to go together, arriving late and leaving early. We hung together outside the gym for an hour, went inside for an hour and then drove home.

I walked through my high school graduation like a mummy tightly wrapped, pale white, bright red lipstick, long black hair like a garish Mexican Day of the Dead figure. Mom was hyperactive as she pushed me around from spot to spot. I mouthed all the appropriate words and accepted my diploma like all the other graduates. I attempted to smile for photos and managed a slight upturn of my lips like Mona Lisa. My friends were fluttering about, smiling, hugging, and laughing. I locked myself into a bathroom stall for as long as I could without getting my mother's undue attention. Mom circulated and Dad spun around the large reception after the ceremony. Oliver stood by my side silently providing me with the role of big sister. My emotional detachment from my little brother hurt terribly as he and I had been allies in the bipolar battles at home. I could do nothing for him now. I felt like crying because he was loyally standing by me even though I had betrayed him by escaping into my own dark world.

Slow as a snail, as the summer days blended together, my depression lifted like the clearing of a thick fog. My appetite returned, my sleep improved, my worries disappeared, my energy returned, my self-esteem rose and I walked again with a bounce in my step. I left the loneliness of my room to rejoin the world. As I noticed myself rising from the land of the living dead, I assumed naively I would never experience that particular brand of despair again. I made no connection between my father's illness and my bout with depression despite my concern that I would be crazy like my father. It was his manic antics that I feared would overtake me causing extremely bad behavior. Whenever I was being loud, silly, carefree, talkative or highly energetic, I feared I was becoming manic. I reined myself in like a runaway horse when the specter of mania passed like a cloud across my consciousness. I feared being too happy as too much happiness might trigger madness. Monitoring my mood became a full time job.

Worrying about my family, monitoring my mood like a mother hen, I got myself together to go off to college. I struggled out of the enmeshed web of my family like a wildly buzzing fly, hoping to survive intact. Dad was too hyper the day I was leaving for college. He barely noted that I was leaving home. Mom, Oliver and I had a big breakfast, loaded my stuff in the trunk and headed for my new home. Boston University buildings ran the strip of land between the ever-busy Commonwealth Avenue and the Charles River. We managed to make only one elevator trip to get my stuff to my dorm room. My roommate seemed cool at first meeting. Mom was funny, doing the introductions. "I'm Molly's mother, this is Oliver, Molly's brother and of course, this is Molly." "How nice to meet you, I'm Janie's mom. This is Janie's father, John." Jane, Oliver and I held our smiles in check over the formality of our parents. I maneuvered my mother and my brother out of the room and led them to the lounge to say my good-byes to them.

The main building on Commonwealth Avenue looked like an aged fortress of cement and iron. The classrooms were overheated and the hallways epitomized boring institutionalism. Students and faculty sparked the dreary surroundings with life in high gear. The newer buildings spiked up like unruly children breaking the heavy architecture. Everything and everyone was stuffed together in this hub of learning. The frequently changing New England weather added significant contributions to the scene. Trolleys clacked by in the middle of the wide avenue discharging and picking up loads of BU people.

I aced my first semester classes and worked my way through second semester with speed and agility. College had set me free from family concerns and given me a world of interesting friends and events. I joined the fast crowd and juggled my studies and my social life like a pro. My contact with my family had been minimal with phone calls from my Mom and Oliver every five or six weeks. Shaking off my family like an old coat led me to believe I was no longer tainted by the bipolar blues. I regretted leaving Oliver back at home in the soup but I was running for my life creating the delusion that I was going to live happily ever after.

Unfortunately, my father was losing his struggle with Bipolar Disorder. His depression over the winter had been severe and he required psychiatric hospitalization for stabilization. Two months after his return home, he cycled into mania. His mania had become complicated by his abuse of alcohol and prescription drugs. He was becoming non-compliant with his treatment. He used downers to knock down from the high of the mania. Under the influence he had crashed his car, luckily not hurting himself or anyone else. He had fallen down the stairs without serious injury. Mom told me he had injected himself with downers in his office and collapsed with the needle in his arm with a waiting room full of patients. Oliver had to tell Dad's patients to go home and call to reschedule. The doctor was indisposed. Oliver then dragged Dad upstairs to his bed, hoping he would revive and not die. Mom had ridden the wave of his affairs, his indiscriminate spending, his drinking and drug use but she was wearing thin.

I maintained the façade of a 'normal' college girl by observing and imitating my peers. I always had something to do and when I didn't have something to do, I found something. My friends thought I was light-hearted, relaxed and always ready for a good time. My classes piqued my interest, my social life buzzed and the academic year flew by. I decided to move into an apartment with two friends when spring semester ended. I landed a summer job in Boston and did not go home except for a weekend visit now and then. When I did go home, my father sat wordlessly in his recliner watching television. He had managed to maintain his office practice and to retain his privileges at the hospital. Mom was back to pretending all was well. We all knew another crisis was inevitable but none of us uttered one single word to indicate we knew. We kept hoping for a cure that never came.

My college years were peppered with recurring incidents of my father's manic behavior drawing me back into the fold of my family. I plowed on in pursuit of my higher education. Oliver went off to college and I breathed a sigh of relief to know he had left the nest relatively unscathed. Mom managed Dad with cajoling and cohersion. Dad bobbed up and down on his bipolar merry-go-round. Miraculously, Dad was able to keep working with time-outs to get his meds tweaked. Mom kept the home fires burning.

I graduated from BU and headed off to New York City to get a Master's Degree in Social Work. I planned to capitalize on the skills I had learned in my family. I was a woman and I was a caretaker. I worried constantly about how others were feeling and if they were doing all right. I tracked everyone's emotional signals, looking for clues as to what might be bothering them and what I could do to help them. Social work was the perfect field for me. I could pick up on what was going on with others and help them identify the areas where they needed help. I was turning a lemon into lemonade.

Life in New York was fast paced and exciting. Caught up in the swirl of the big city, I opened to new possibilities. I developed a new sense of freedom although I continued to worry about my family. The imprint of my family would remain with me always. My dream of forging an independent life seemed to be coming true until my phone rang in the middle of the night. I answered to my Mom's voice running in my ear in a garbled stream of words. I pulled out the essence from her excited monologue. It would seem my brother Oliver was in a psychiatric hospital. He was brought to the ER by the police when he jumped out on the roof and screamed he had been poisoned. He had no drugs on board and was admitted to the psychiatric floor.

"I'm on my way, Mom."

I got the first flight to Boston. Mom met me at the airport and we drove to the hospital in silence. In the foyer to the psychiatric unit, we signed in and sat in the waiting room. We were admitted to the unit by a burly man carrying a big ring of keys who led us to a large room with tables and chairs. We sat until Oliver shuffled into the room. I gave him a hug. He didn't hug me back but followed me to sit next to Mom.

"I came against my will. They strapped me down and took my shoes away. Get me out of here! They're poisoning me. The food is poisoned. They shot me up with poison. I have to use my sixth sense to stop the poison from killing me. Please take me home with you," Oliver said.

Mom looked at me like a deer in headlights.

"Oliver, we can't take you home today. No one is poisoning you. No one wants to hurt you. These people want to help you. They have been very nice to Mom and me and they want to help you. The doctors and nurses here at the hospital will help you come home if you let them help you. You need to eat the food and you need to take the medication to get better."

"No, I have to get out of here. I have to get out. Please, Molly!"

"Oliver, you are tired and sick right now. You need to stay here and rest and take care of yourself."

"Oliver, please listen to Molly. She is telling you the truth. She has no reason to lie to you."

"No, I have to get out of here. If I stay here, I'll die. Don't you understand? I'll die."

"Oliver, you are not going to die. You are safe here. If you don't stop talking about dying, Mom and I will have to leave now and let you rest. We'll have to leave you now and come back when you are rested."

"No, I have to get home. Dad wants me to come home. He needs me. He'll drive off the road and get killed. I have to drive him. Mom will get killed too. Make these people understand, I have a job to do!"

"Dad will be fine, Oliver. Mom will be fine, too. Dad wants you to let the doctors help you. When the doctors have helped you, you can come home and help him."

"No, Molly, help me get out now!"

Oliver slumped in his seat. His paranoid delusions were entrenched. I reassured him that he was safe, that he was in a good place and that he needed to take the medicine. If he took the medicine, he would get better and come home. Nothing I said changed his distorted thinking. Mom and I decided to leave. We hugged Oliver good-bye. I turned to wave to him from the entrance but he was occupied with his internal drama and did not notice me. Tears streamed down my face on the seemingly endless drive to my parents' house from the hospital. I had lost another family member to mental illness. I could not believe my little brother had become so ill. I could not believe it.

Oliver had traveled to another dimension. Oliver's psychosis was dramatic and debilitating. He would require a lengthy recuperation and ongoing supportive care. The image of my brother in the hospital inserted itself into my mind's eye. Another blast of mental illness had struck like a tornado, leaving destruction in its wake. My sweet, sensitive brother had been transformed into a mental patient. I rode my own waves of sadness, anger, denial, shock and fatigue.

"Oh, Molly, I cannot believe Oliver is sick. It's too much to imagine," Mom said as we arrived home.

Next day, I visited Oliver on his unit. Mom and Dad were paralyzed with grief. I told them to rest at home. I'd visit Oliver at the hospital.

"I'm taking the pills, Molly, I met a guy here and he tells me the pills are good. The pills won't hurt me, he said. He said he's leaving in a few days because he takes the pills. He said you can stop taking the pills when you get out. So I'll take the pills so I can get out and then I'll stop taking them."

"It's great that you're taking the pills. Please keep taking the pills, Oliver, until the doctor tells you to stop because if you stop on your own, you will end up back here in the hospital. If you want to stay out of the hospital, keep taking the pills."

I wondered how Oliver would manage. What limits and challenges might he have? I couldn't believe his life was transformed so suddenly from success in school with a circle of friends to his current level of hospitalization. He'd received a life sentence without parole. Madness can be held at bay like barking dogs or faced full on, no more running, no more hiding. Most minds never journey from reality but some minds do. The next day, when I visited Oliver at the hospital, he kept referring to his childhood events as the reason for his problems. The meds were starting to work and he was trying to understand what had happened to him, blaming the events in his childhood. He would need psychiatric care to begin to understand.

The next day, I visited Oliver with my father and my mother. Oliver was becoming more coherent and more grounded in reality. Dad was depressed. He had passed on Bipolar Disorder to his son, a hard fact to accept and assimilate. Dad told Oliver to listen to the doctors and he would be able to come home soon. Oliver seemed to take in Dad's message. Mom asked Oliver questions about his activities, his eating and sleeping. Oliver was participating in his treatment, eating and sleeping more. We played cards. I said my good-byes to Oliver as I was flying back to New York. I had brought him several books to read. I promised I'd be back to see him soon.

When I returned to New York, I threw myself into the final throes of my graduate program. I kept in touch by phone with my parents and with Oliver. Mom's distress oozed over the telephone. Dad was depressed and wouldn't come to the phone to talk to me. Oliver's psychosis was controlled with meds but he was deeply depressed. When Oliver was discharged from the hospital, Mom invited me to come home for a visit. Oliver was sleeping when I arrived at my parents' home. When Mom sent me to wake Oliver for dinner, Oliver woke and looked at me as if he didn't know me. My brother had turned into a zombie. He didn't know me and I didn't know him. He was lethargic with a glazed look in his eyes.

"Oliver, it's time for dinner."

He was no longer Oliver. In his place, a new Oliver had emerged. The new Oliver didn't smile, laugh or cry. The new Oliver walked with a careful gait. The new Oliver didn't make eye contact or pay attention to what people said to him. Oliver acted out. He fought with Dad, cursed at Dad, slammed doors, threw things, yelled and stomped around the house. My attempts to engage him in conversation were fruitless. He watched TV, slept a lot and refused to leave the house. Mom was jacked up on denial but despair coated her like slime. Dad sat depressed and mute in front of the TV. Oliver sat depressed and mute with a glazed look at the other end of the sofa, a younger version of Dad. I plopped down between them and started chatting, casting about for a subject that might engage any and all of my family members. Mom responded to me and we continued our idle chatter in an effort to keep a flame of hope alive in the darkness.

The weekend jerked to an end. I reached out to hug Dad and Oliver good-bye. Mom and I struggled with our tears as I hugged her good-bye. I returned to New York like a rat deserting a sinking ship. My life in New York marched on leading to a job as a hospital social worker. Always in the back of my mind like a tune that wouldn't quit was my family in Boston playing out the bipolar drama. I pretended I really had a normal family back home but Mom's calls punctured my tale of fiction. I drifted into guilt and shame, feeling powerless and hopeless. I started throwing myself into romantic episodes to avoid dealing with despair about my father and brother. In college, I had wanted to be like everyone else and had imitated the frantic dating patterns of my peers. Now, my friends were settling down, having 'serious' relationships, even having babies. I didn't want anything 'serious', preferring serial 'romance' with the highs and lows. Relationships were another planet, light years away.

But when I met Alex, I never imagined we would be anything beyond good friends. We hung out together and slowly became lovers without any alarm bells going off in my head. Alex was finishing up his last rotation in medical school. I was finishing up my program internship as an ER social worker. We cruised along weaving our lives together, making time in our busy schedules for 'special' time. When Alex asked me to live with him, I agreed before I could think about it. After I agreed, I was riddled with second thoughts but managed to calm myself down with Alex's help. We found a reasonable place to live, moved in quickly and got back to work.

I had told Alex my family story a number of times and he was familiar with all the players. I warned him of the chaos created by my dad and brother. Alex reassured me that he could handle it. It didn't take long before he was put to the test. I was beached by a call from my mother telling me my father had been in a car accident. Dad was in critical condition. I flew to Boston with Alex. Mom greeted us in the ICU. She looked horrible. She felt like rigor mortis had set in when I hugged her. I introduced her to Alex. Alex was meeting my parents for the first time on the intensive care unit. Alex helped us get settled and then went off to get coffee, water and food. Mom started to cry. I held her hand and waited for her to update me on Dad's condition.

"He drove off the road, hit a tree, broke two ribs, punctured left lung, broken left arm."

We sat in silence.

"Dad's been manic for weeks," Mom said.

"Why didn't you let me know?"

"I didn't want to bother you. You're so busy."

"I'm here now. Have the doctors told you what's going on with Dad now?"

"He's not breathing on his own. That's what they told me first thing this morning. I need to tell Oliver about Dad. I haven't told him yet. I was hoping you could help me tell him about Dad."

"All right! Let's meet him at a nearby café and tell him."

Mom and I left the hospital to meet Oliver at a coffee place near the hospital. Alex stayed at the hospital to call us if anything happened with Dad. We met Oliver, ordered, sat down and I told Oliver about Dad as gently as I could. I couldn't change the fact that Dad's life was on the line. I listed the superlative qualities of the hospital but Oliver knew what our family was facing. We had faced this possibility throughout our lives. Oliver cried, we all cried, finished our coffee and headed to the hospital.

Oliver and I walked into Dad's room and stood amidst the tubes, wires, monitors and IV bags that hang around Dad like Xmas tree decorations. Oliver was silently crying. I reached over and held his hand. We stood upright by Dad's bedside until a nurse signaled us to leave. When we rejoined Mom and Alex in the waiting room, an eternity passed before the doctor gave us good news. Dad was able to breathe without support and his prognosis was good. Nobody mentioned his mania. Nobody mentioned the possibility of suicidal depression. Dad would live to cycle again.

Back in New York, I worked like a maniac and loved like a fool. Alex and I visited my family when my father was discharged from the hospital. We all pretended everything was fine but back home in New York, intrusive thoughts of my family's mess woke me every night at three in the morning. I learned to meditate. If I absolutely could not get back to sleep, I'd bug Alex until he woke and we would mess around. Alex had made himself indispensible, my man of the hour. I had thought when Alex met my family I'd be saying good-bye to him but to my surprise, Alex liked my family and they liked him. I knew my family members had wonderful attributes but lost sight of their strengths in my swirl of fear and helplessness. Alex helped me to see the good stuff and maintain emotional equilibrium in face of the bad stuff.

Like a gift from the vacation gods, Alex and I were able to wiggle around our schedules to cover other staff members' shifts in order to have three days off at the same time. Alex suggested we visit his family in southern California. Alarm bells clanged in my head. Family was associated with crisis for me. Family meant sinking into quicksand. I was reluctant to meet or make a family as my struggle out of the bog of my family had been perilous. Once I calmed down, I was able to envision a different kind of family with the hope that Alex and I could create our own healthy family. We made our visit to La Jolla, a seaside city embedded in the cliffs above the Pacific Ocean near San Diego. We stayed at Alex parents' place in the guest wing. I met his father Tom, his mother Kate and his sister Kristie who were easy-going and welcomed me with open arms. We had a great time sight-seeing, surfing and eating delicious food. Alex's family bore no resemblance to my family. I felt happy but I could not trust it. Something would happen to take it away. Something always did.

Months later, Alex and I decided to marry at City Hall. Family events tended to stir up stress for my family and the distance for Alex's family created a challenge. One sunny Monday morning, we woke up and decided to get married without fanfare. I couldn't have done it any other way. We had coffee, went to city hall, got our marriage license and waited in line with the other couples for our turn to say our vows to the clerk who then stamped our license. We were married. At home, we made our favorite breakfast, opened a bottle of champagne and ate and drank with gusto. Next day, we phoned our parents and broke the news. We made plans for a joint family gathering over Labor Day to celebrate our union with our families comingled.

Being married changed little as we bounced back to work and our life together. We teased each other about Mrs. and Mr. and our friends teased us too. It changed when we started talking about having kids. Alex wanted at least two kids. I hadn't given it much thought except that I worried about passing the bipolar gene to future generations. Alex reassured me that it was worth taking the chance. I decided I didn't want to forgo having a family out of fear of having kids with bipolar. After all, my father, in spite of his bipolar diagnosis, succeeded at becoming a physician and helping lots of people. My brother when stable strived to have a normal life. Oliver had friends, a job driving taxi and had taken up photography.

As each day passed in joy, possibilities opened in my mind. I became less anxious and more hopeful. I threw caution to the wind and became pregnant several months later. I passed my pregnancy in a pink cloud full of energy and optimism. The 'hormone bath' as my mother called it, made me feel happier than I had ever felt. Alex told me I was made to have children. The high started fading by the beginning of my eighth month with a sore lower back, swollen feet, fatigue and crankiness. I stopped working, stayed home, took gentle strolls around the city and spent time with my feet up. As I was adapting to my status as a very pregnant woman, I started labor and off I went to the birthing room at the hospital.

Seven hours later, my baby girl was placed in my arms. I felt a rush of love as I looked into my newborn infant's eyes and saw love and trust radiating toward me in baby waves. Annie was beautiful, perfect, an angel, a six-pound bundle of dark hair, brown eyes, pinkish-white skin, little bow-shaped mouth, little round face, little nose, little hands and feet. She was all new. Alex, Annie and I cuddled in the hospital bed, nuzzling and muzzling with each other in our own little world.

"Life is glorious," I sang to Annie and Alex.

"Look at our precious little girl, Molly!"

I held Annie up to my face making cooing sounds. She was wrapped snuggly in her soft flannels with a little hat on her head. Her eyes locked with my eyes and I became lost in our private, wordless world. After I nursed her, Alex walked her around the room, talking to her in baby talk.

"Molly, Molly, Annie looks as if she knows everything."

"I know, Alex, that's exactly what I was thinking. She knows everything she needs to know."

Alex and I cuddled with Annie, expecting our happiness to continue forever.

Being hit hard by postpartum depression came out of the blue and threw me down the stairs. The symptoms of depression came roaring in like a fierce hurricane and knocked the new mother down. My brain chemistry was screwed up crashing down on my head like shattered glass. Although interruptions in sleep are a pre-requisite to caring for an infant, I could not sleep at all. My sleep cycle was screwed up in a big way and my exhaustion hastened my downward spiral. I didn't feel hungry and started losing weight. I didn't bother getting dressed but wore my pajamas all day. I avoided people and had trouble concentrating. I lost my sense of joy in my precious new baby.

I thought I might have 'baby blues' but my weeping spells kept increasing. The emotional pain was unbearable and I began to have suicidal thoughts. I struggled with my ominous thoughts and my desperate feelings. I forced myself out of bed to take care of Annie and lay in bed with her while she slept. Intellectually, I knew I was suffering from clinical depression but the depression had overtaken so completely, I lost sight of normal. I thought I was totally worthless and deserved to suffer. I didn't know what horrible crime I had committed but I knew I was guilty. My very existence was a mistake which could only be remedied by ending my life. Emotional pain wracked me with such ferocity I thought I had to end my life to escape the pain. There was no other way.

I fought the thoughts of suicide, trying to reason with myself. I told myself: "I am a mother. I must take care of my daughter. I love my daughter. What kind of mother would abandon her baby by committing suicide?" Depression answered, "Your baby would be better off without you." I berated myself for being a terrible mother. I could not win an argument with depression. The perverse illogical process of my depressed brain was trying to kill me and I knew that depression kills.

Alex and I shared our concerns about my being caught up by postpartum depression. My suicidal ideation convinced us both that I needed to consult a psychiatrist.

"It's the smart thing do to, Mol. No need to continue suffering. Many new mothers develop postpartum depression. Humans started out in tribes with more support for mothers after giving birth. Now we keep mothers and babies healthier but we send them home to a nuclear family and expect all to be bliss and bubbles."

"Alex, you are cute. Your theories are fascinating to be sure but I'm going under, even with all your help. I don't care if this depression is biochemical, evolutionary or karmic. I just want it to go away and go away quickly."

"I'll schedule an appointment with a shrink right now. Do you know anyone you want to see?"

"I've heard that Amy Weiss is good."

"I'm on it."

Each day was worse than the day before. Depression was eroding me geometrically day by day. My scheduled appointment with the psychiatrist seemed light years away and I doubted that anything could help me. It was too late. I had concluded there was no escape from the unremitting despair that had overtaken me. I continued to reside in my body but I was dead.

The psychiatric appointment day finally arrived with Alex, Annie and I getting to Dr. Weiss' office early. Every depression has its own story and I narrated mine to Dr. Amy Weiss as tears streamed down my face. Dr. Weiss listened attentively as I muddled along recounting my family history of Bipolar Disorder, my visit and return from depression at the end of my senior year of high school and my current topple into the Grand Canyon of depression. Alex sat quietly by my side, holding my hand. Annie was asleep in her carrier at our feet.

Dr. Weiss questioned me about my thoughts of suicide, "Have you made any plans to commit suicide, Molly?"

"I've thought of taking an overdose of pills, filling the bathtub, getting in and drowning but I can't leave Annie and Alex."

"Have you made a suicide attempt?"

"No, I can't do it. Part of me knows my suicidal thoughts are a symptom of postpartum depression. Knowing that helps me fight off the thoughts of killing myself. They pop up like mushrooms at the strangest time. I understand the expression 'losing my mind'. My thoughts are out of my control."

"Molly, are you having strange or bizarre thoughts?"

"No, I'm not."

"Is it all right if I ask Alex for his impressions?"

"Yes."

"Alex?"

"Molly is toughing out her depressive symptoms. She's not eating, not sleeping. She's depleted, worn out, anxious, depressed and doing her best to carry on. She's not psychotic and I don't believe she has taken any action to hurt herself. She is doing a great job even if she doesn't think so," Alex said.

"Molly, as you know, depression is treatable with antidepressants. How would you feel about giving up breastfeeding your baby?"

"I would like to keep breastfeeding her," I said.

"Taking antidepressants will improve your mood and help you be more emotionally available to Annie but you would have to stop breastfeeding," Dr. Weiss said.

"I guess I could stop."

"Depression robs people of their power. It's the nature of the disease. By choosing to treat your depression, you would be empowering yourself. I'm concerned about your symptoms especially the suicidal ideation. What do you think, Molly?" Dr. Weiss said.

A small amount of relief trickled through me as I listened to Dr. Weiss' words. I longed to sleep and never wake up. I thought of my father attempting to hang himself when he was my age. The obsession to kill myself seemed more than I could handle. I thought of my explanation to patients and family members when working at the hospital. Depression is a disorder of the brain and responds to treatment. I needed treatment and Dr. Weiss was recommending taking antidepressants and a medication for sleep.

I started to cry as a wave of searing emotional pain attacked me. I truly understood why mental illness is called 'emotional disturbance'. I felt too weak to move, too hopeless to hope treatment could help me.

"I'll start medication," I said but I did not feel empowered.

Dr. Amy Weiss sent me home with prescriptions for an antidepressant and a sleep aid. She explained that antidepressants take a week or two to work effectively and up to a month or more to completely relieve symptoms of depression. She prescribed starting at a low dose, increasing the dosage gradually until I would be taking a full dose. I took the anti-depressant as soon as we arrived home. Alex trundled me off to bed.

"Molly, try to rest now! You may be able to sleep. I'm going to care for Annie until you get up. Don't worry about us! We will be having a great time."

"O.K, Alex, thanks," I said as I crawled into bed. I felt hopeful for the first time in weeks. I managed a few hours of sleep. Alex and Annie were in bed with me when I awoke. Annie was tucked into the crook of Alex's arm sleeping as Alex read a medical journal.

"Molly, you're awake!" Alex whispered to me.

"I slept. Seems like a miracle to sleep."

"Are you hungry? I made a veggie casserole."

Before I could answer, Alex headed to the kitchen with Annie in his arms. I joined them and held Annie while Alex heated a serving of dinner for me. I had some of the food and drank a glass of milk.

"I feel like I can breathe again with relief on the horizon. How's Annie doing with the bottle?"

"She's doing great. She guzzles the milk with no problems. She'll be fine."

I looked at my sleeping baby and prayed the pills would bring me back to her before too long. Taking the sleep aid at bedtime, I slept for seven hours, waking groggy and disoriented. Alex had tended Annie all night giving my body, mind and soul a chance to mend. I felt guilty because Alex had to take on my responsibilities.

"I'm sorry, Alex. I want to take care of Annie and be available for you too."

"Molly, think about it. If I had an illness, you would take care of me and Annie. You can't help being sick and you're doing all the right things to get better. Feeling guilty is not going to help your recovery, so let it go! If it gets too much for me, we'll talk and get some help. For right now, I'm good."

Alex stayed home with Annie and me for three weeks until the antidepressants did the trick of lifting me from the depths of despair in a steady upward trajectory toward a normal mood. With increased serotonin shining in my brain, I started to look forward to the future. Mending like a cracked limb, I got back on my feet by the end of six weeks. I recovered from the big 'D' and forgot just how horrible I had felt having my brain screech to a grinding halt and throw me under the bus. Or feeling better, I didn't want to remember.

I could have kissed Dr. Amy Weiss, I really could. She had helped me so much. I was dependent on medication to function fully and I didn't care. All I cared was that antidepressants were available and that they worked for me. Dr. Amy Weiss assured me my meds would continue to work for me until I was well enough to taper off them. I believed Dr. Amy Weiss.

Our nervous systems are like delicately tuned many stringed instruments and the climate can loosen, tighten or just plain pop our strings. I thought I was playing beautiful music as I tapered off my antidepressants following nine months of well-modulated mood but I was becoming manic. Alex was surprised to see me awake at four in the morning painting a mural in the hallway.

"Holy cow, Molly! What are you doing?"

"Painting a mural."

"It has a certain appeal."

"When I finish the mural, I'm going to plant a garden on the balcony. I have a lot of energy and haven't felt so creative in a long time. I want to help people realize the importance of preserving nature."

"You are popping with ideas, aren't you?"

I continued at my fevered pitch for several weeks. Alex suggested that I move up my appointment with Dr. Amy Weiss.

"Why? I'm feeling fine. I'm going shopping with Annie to buy her some new outfits and toys. Then I'm meeting Julie and Toby at the park for a play date. Then I'm doing the grocery shopping. I want to make a new Middle Eastern dish. Do you want me to pick up anything for you?"

"Molly, you've had a few buying sprees recently. You've been running around like a maniac, with the emphasis on 'mania' in maniac. We're having lots of sex, a real high for us with the emphasis on the word 'high'.

"Alex, are you suggesting I'm 'manic'? I'm tapering off my meds and re-adjusting. I feel good and you're diagnosing me?"

"You're right, I should not be diagnosing you but will you see Dr. Weiss earlier than scheduled?"

I had noticed my decreased amount of sleep, my increased amount of socializing and my feelings of euphoria but I thought I was normal, only happier than usual. I agreed to see Dr. Amy Weiss earlier than my scheduled appointment. Imagine my surprise when she told me I was hypomanic.

"No, I'm feeling great and getting lots of things done at home and at work. I think the antidepressants were flattening my mood and now without them, I'm coming back to normal," I said.

"Do you object to my hearing from Alex?" Dr. Weiss asked.

"Have you and Alex been talking about me?"

"No, I have not talked with Alex. I believe your mood is elevated. I would like to hear Alex's observations."

I gestured towards Alex and prepared for his assessment of my mood and behavior. I liked how I was feeling and wanted to continue feeling 'elevated'.

"Molly has been active, engaged in multiple and overlapping projects. She comes to bed after midnight and gets up early in the morning. She's painting a mural in our hallway. She's been going out to see her friends frequently. She's back to work full-time and keeps on working when she gets home. She's been buying and bringing home lots of new things for all of us."

"Molly, hypomania is unusual when tapering off antidepressants. It's a paradoxical response. I'm changing your diagnosis to Bipolar Disorder. I want to monitor you closely as you continue to taper off. I want to start you on a medication at bedtime to help you to go to sleep earlier and to sleep through the night."

I agreed to Dr. Weiss recommendations and slept well that night. Slowly as several weeks passed, the energy and drive of hypomania dissipated.

On my next visit, Dr. Amy Weiss pronounced me 'stable'. My mood was normal, neither high nor low.

"Molly, I'd like to see you in three weeks. You are well but I'd like to stay in touch.

I continued to see Dr. Weiss for three months and stopped seeing her as my mood remained normal. She cautioned me that I might have post-partum depression again. She advised me to seek psychiatric care if pregnant.

"What are the chances I'll continue having mood cycles?"

"That is hard to predict, Molly. See me or another psychiatrist if you suspect you are experiencing clinical depression or hypomania. Psychotherapy could be helpful for you. I can give you referrals."

"My whole family is bipolar. What are Annie's chances of inheriting this disease?"

"That is difficult to predict. Watch her closely and intervene early if she seems to have symptoms!"

I planned to watch Annie very closely. Alex reassured me with a list of the great things people with Bipolar Disorder have done, including the mural I painted in the hallway. I could not be lulled into a false sense of hope having experienced bipolar cycles as a family member and as a patient. I didn't think anyone who had not been exposed to people suffering from Bipolar Disorder could understand the anxiety and helplessness engendered by abnormal mood swings and unpredictable behavior. Having dipped into depression myself with its attendant feelings of despair, worthlessness, its energy draining suction and its creation of thoughts of suicide followed by a swing up to hypomania with its extreme energy, affirmation of life and tremendous self-confidence, I knew how hard it might be for others to understand.

I settled into a routine life of normal ups and downs. I wrapped myself into my life and within months, my adventures in Bipolar Land became distant and denied memories. After Alex and I talked and agreed, I cut back my job to half time to spend more time with Annie. Leaving her with the baby-sitter tugged too hard at my heart and made me worry too much at work. My life revolved around my little girl and it had become increasingly hard to leave her. I marveled at the powerful feelings attached to motherhood as I morphed from a rather self-centered young adult to a woman focused on the needs of a very small person.

As Alex neared the completion of his residency, he was offered his dream job: a clinical-research combo at Mass General. Alex sealed the deal and we started planning to move to Boston. I put thoughts of the move on a back burner but Alex kept me on task as the move grew closer. The day of the move was rapidly approaching. As I came in the door to our apartment with Annie in my arms, the telephone drew my attention from Annie's rendition of 'Twinkle, Twinkle Little Star'. Annie, a rocking two year-old with lots of moves, wiggled out of my arms when I plunked her down in the living room.

"Hello."

"Molly, you will never guess what! You will not believe this!"

"What, Mom?" I said as I pulled off Annie's jacket and found a toy for her.

"Oliver has found a new job with better pay."

"That's great, Mom. What's the new job?" I said as I played with Annie.

"He landed a job as an insurance adjuster."

"Great!"

"Are you finished packing?"

"I'm almost finished with lots of odds and ends to do."

"Let's get together as soon as you're settled," Mom said before she hung up.

Alex wouldn't be home until later. I fed, bathed and got Annie to bed. Annie quickly fell asleep, tucked into our big bed with her pink pajamas. She was the portrait of serenity, dark curls tumbling over her still face. I wanted to curl up beside her, close my eyes and drift into darkness. I shook off my fatigue and plugged away at putting the final touches to our departure.

Alex's new position in Boston started in ten days. We were moving to Boston tomorrow. The past two years had been busy and beautiful. Annie, the center of the family, got us up every day and put us to sleep every night. Thinking of leaving my first home with Alex and Annie sent waves of anxiety along my neural network. Alex and I had moved into this apartment together. The open floor plan, the parquet floors, two bedrooms, two baths, easy walking distance to a park, the shops and the subway stop had made the apartment ideal for us. Nesting in the apartment during my pregnancy had given me a new sense of peace and joy. Alex and I had prepared the baby's room with special attention to every detail. Bringing Annie home from the hospital to the apartment was a well-documented affair. Tears, laughter, tenderness and fatigue were captured for future viewing. Annie's album was filled with photos of dyads, triads and groups gathered around her.

I had become aware of the depth of my attachment to the apartment when the plan to move to Boston started to coalesce. Moving back to Boston would be a challenge of significance for me. Living near my family would pull me back into their orbit. Mom ran on high anxiety. Dad's mood was unpredictable and Oliver's condition was fluid. I had monitored my family members' ups and downs from New York. Now I'd be center stage for all the action.

Helping out was programmed into me like the freckles on my face. Trouble knocked me down around my family because I helped out, helped out and helped out until I was in need of help myself. I would worry, fret and try to control unmanageable situations until frazzled. The madness never stopped and I kept trying to stop the flow of the raging river. I had learned tools of self-care like mindfulness, setting boundaries and asking others for help but in the midst of my family drama, my brain rewound to the old days of fear and helplessness and then I became no good for anybody. Alex and my friends tried to convince me that the progress I had made in my life since leaving home would inoculate me against family dysfunction.

Annie whimpered in her sleep. I curled up around her on the bed. Annie was good medicine. I would do anything for her. I planned to manage my stress, put her needs at the top of my list and seek treatment immediately if my mood crumbled. Forewarned was forearmed and I was prepared for battle. I fell asleep and awoke when Alex slipped in next to me. We whispered a few sweet nothings and fell asleep. We were both exhausted with the tasks of finishing up at our jobs and preparing for our new life in Boston. Tomorrow was the big day.

I woke up alone in our big bed. I heard Annie and Alex in the kitchen. I stumbled in, poured coffee and plopped into a chair across from Annie in her high chair.

"Rise and shine, Queen of Hearts! The Princess and I have been awake for hours," Alex said.

21

"The movers will be here in fifteen minutes. Why didn't you wake me up? You are coddling me, you sweet thing."

"Mol, you looked so content sleeping on your pink satin pillow. Let's face it, I owe you big time. Moving back to Boston is not on your 'to do' list, yet like a devoted spouse, you are making the sacrifice for my career."

"I would do anything for my spouse."

"Anything! Really?"

Alex reached his hand across the table and took mine. We shared a meaningful look at which point Annie threw her cereal bowl on the floor.

"The Princess is displeased," Alex said.

"Annie," I said, trying not to smile, "throwing food on the floor is not O.K. Can you use your words and tell me what you want?" I said.

"Mommy, I want Mommy."

I took Annie into my lap and cuddled her until she became restless and slid down. Picking up the food from the floor, I mentally steeled myself for moving day. The movers arrived and within a few hours our apartment was stripped of all our belongings. Annie enjoyed running through the empty rooms.

"Annie, let's go get in the car," I said.

"Boston, here we come," Alex said as we left our apartment for good.

In our new apartment in Boston, we started our new life. Alex settled into his new job with new colleagues and shared his adventures with me and Annie every evening over dinner. I enjoyed being a full-time mom and homemaker. I met other mothers with small children and soon had a schedule of activities for stroller walks, park playtime, mommy and me classes and just plain hanging-out with the moms and the kids. Alex and I decided to try for another child and it didn't take long before Eliza came along.

"Oh, sweet Susanna," Alex sang in the shower. I cuddled Eliza while Annie jumped on the bed with vigor.

"Annie, honey, sit on the bed! Beds are not for jumping."

"I'll fly off the bed," she said as she jumped from the bed to the floor landing on her feet, tumbling over on the rug. Annie laughed as she rolled over a few times.

"Stop feeding the baby, Mommy! I'm hungry."

"O.K., Annie, do you want oatmeal with milk or eggs with toast for breakfast?"

"I want oatmeal and baby sister wants oatmeal too."

"Eliza's too little to eat oatmeal. I'll make oatmeal for you, big girl. Do you want to help me cook the oatmeal?"

Even though incredibly sleep-deprived, I was filled with happiness. Alex and our two girls gave my life a sense of fullness. Alex's gentle care of me and the girls made me believe in good outcomes and happy families. Alex was happy, too. We were both exhausted from lack of sleep but we laughed, played and cuddled together with Annie. Days and nights passed like a vacation in heaven. Love was growing exponentially in my immediate family but I was feeling a downward drift in mood. I was in love with my life yet the dark rumble of impending despair was present in the far reaches of my brain. My insight into the 'insanity' of becoming depressed when all was well in my world helped me develop compassion for my father who would throw away his family members and his achievements like trash when the rumblings of his bipolar storms claimed the circuitry of his brain. When his brain chemistry returned to normal, he faced the dire consequences of his abnormal behavior while he was ill.

I didn't wait until I was in a full-blown depression before I started taking medication again. Taking antidepressants before I sank into a black hole was a good move. I wished I didn't have to stop breastfeeding Eliza but I knew if I sank into depression, I would not be available to care for her. I had no choice. I was rewarded by a robust response to the antidepressant and a rapid return to a normal mood. I set my schedule around the kids' needs and eked out enough time to maintain my mood. Annie started preschool and looked forward to her school days. Alex came home and played with the kids while I prepared dinner. We ate, played, bathed the kids, helped the kids go to sleep and did adult things until Eliza woke for her feeding. Life was back to normal again with the sweet addition of Eliza.

The only blot on the sun for me was dealing with my parents. My mother had advice for me on all aspects of my life. She visited me on a weekly basis and started making lists for me to do. I asked her for practical, immediate help but she graciously declined. Grand gestures gave her pleasure like buying expensive dresses for the girls, equipping her house with top of the line expensive baby furniture and hiring an expensive photographer to photograph the girls. My mother liked to keep up appearances. My father struggled to maintain a good appearance even though his life force was waning as was evident by his lack of energy and poor health. He continued to practice medicine as a staff physician at a state hospital. His mood was subdued when he visited me and the girls with Mom.

I placed the sweet pink bundle of Eliza in Dad's arms. She was quiet, looking up at him with her big baby blue eyes.

"Do you remember when I was this little, Dad?"

"I do remember," he said in a soft voice.

"You were never that small, Molly," Mom interjected. "Or that cute," she tagged on.

I practiced ignoring Mom's insults. I worried that she had endured too much to be happy. Alex was at the hospital and would not return home for hours. My parents might visit for hours. Annie provided an entertaining distraction with her conversation and antics. Annie brought one of her books to her grandmother, climbed on her lap and commanded her to read. We were quiet as Annie listened raptly to the story of rabbits and rainbows. Annie jumped down at the end of the story and returned to her grandmother with another of her books to be read. I knew Annie would present each of her many books to her grandmother to be read to her. Annie's attention span for her books was remarkable. Mentally, I prepared for Annie to have a melt-down if her grandmother refused to read every one of her books to her. Not much would distract Annie from her disappointment.

My plan was to head off disruption by taking over the book reading when I sensed my Mom was ready for a break. As a result of my bipolar upbringing, I was keenly attuned to the energy and signals of others. I sensed my mother's drop in enthusiasm with reading to Annie. As Annie picked up another book, I offered to read to her. I sat beside her and reached out for the book she was offering to her grandmother.

"No, Grandma reads the book!" Annie said with the look of early childhood defiance. A year ago, she might have had a tantrum but being older she would allow for negotiation and compromise, I hoped.

"Annie, you are such a big girl. Please let me read your book to you. Grandma wants to go potty. Right, Grandma? Don't you need to go to the bathroom now?"

"How did you know I need to go to the bathroom, Molly? I do need to go to the bathroom."

'Going potty' was a sacred ritual to Annie. She immediately jumped off the sofa and headed for the hallway to the bathroom.

"Mom, Annie will come back here if you go into the bathroom alone and close the door."

Annie ran back to the living room. "Grandma goes potty alone."

"That's right, Annie, grown-ups like to go potty alone."

"Do you like to go potty alone, Grandpa?"

"Yes, Annie, I like to go alone. I like privacy."

"I don't like to go alone. I like Mommy or Daddy to go with me," Annie said.

"When you are a bigger girl, you will like to go alone to the bathroom."

"O.K.", Annie said as she handed me her book to read.

Mom returned from the bathroom and I stood to attention automatically. My nervous system reacted to each of my parents in different ways. I was on guard with my mother and wanted to appease her, please her and make her happy. My father elicited sadness in me when he was depressed and high anxiety when he was manic. If he was cruising in the middle ground, I remained neutral but alert for any shift in his mood. I felt trapped in my home with my parents, making attempts to protect my two little girls. I hoped I was not transmitting my tangle of emotions to them. I felt myself fragmenting, abandoning my own position to accommodate to the interests of the others in the room. I wanted to scoop up Annie and Eliza and run from my home to take them to a safe place.

"Molly, can we take you and the girls out to lunch?" Dad said.

"Lunch sounds delightful. I haven't been out for lunch too often with the girls. Would you want to go to Pinky's for lunch? Pinky's is child-friendly with a nice playground," I said.

"Pinky's, Pinky's, I want Pinky's," Annie said.

"Pinky's won't have anything I want to eat," Mom said.

"Where do you want to go, Mom?" I asked.

"Yes, where do you want to go?" Dad asked Mom.

"Pinky's, Pinky's, I want Pinky's," Annie said.

"Yes, Annie, you want Pinky's. Grandma wants to go to another great place. Where do you want to go, Grandma?" I said.

"I'd like to go to Manga's. Get the girls presentable and we'll go to Manga's! Change your clothes, too!"

"OK," I said as I rose to do as she commanded.

I ushered the girls into their room to get them ready to go to Manga's.

In the parking lot at Manga's, after trying to eat a salad while holding Eliza, except when my father held her briefly and chasing Annie around the large room filled with adults, I said my good-byes to my parents, hooked the kids into their car seats, drove home and collapsed onto the sofa. Fortunately the kids were tired too and slept, giving me respite until Alex came home from work to find me resting on the sofa with Eliza sleeping in the crook of my arm and Annie asleep tucked under her blanket on the love seat. I pulled my feet up for him to sit on the sofa. He moved up alongside me and nuzzled my neck. I turned to kiss him as Eliza started to make waking-up sounds. I sat up to soothe Eliza, holding her in one arm and Alex in the other. Annie slept on.

Months later, without warning, life dealt me a big whammy. Emotional pain swept over me like a tidal wave as tears and sobs bubbled up and erupted outward. Whipping through disbelief, tears, anger and anguish and then back to disbelief, I was spinning in a new emotional territory. Dad was dead. His death was quick and I prayed painless. He had died of a heart attack. Oliver and I were numb. Mom was hyperactive. Oliver, Mom and I sat around the table at my parents' house eating Chinese take-out, our first family dinner without Dad in silence. Mom broke the silence with her 'to do' list. Oliver and I split the tasks and got to work.

The Memorial was Saturday. I kissed Alex and the girls as I left to pick up Oliver in the morning. Oliver talked to me about his feelings of grief and cried as he spoke of his regret. Since Oliver's breakdown, the course of his interactions with Dad had been littered with arguments, rejections and recriminations followed by reunions. I shared with Oliver my regrets about blaming Dad for my problems as if Dad had chosen to be born with Bipolar Disorder. I had let my anger about his bad bipolar behavior create a barrier between us. The barrier had crumbled with his death and guilt was raking my heart. We commiserated on our inability to have at least one last talk with Dad to apologize and share our love with him.

The Memorial brought a lot of people Dad had known and helped. His reputation had been tarnished by his bipolar antics but in spite of his misdoings, he was well-liked. His skills and compassion waned at the extreme poles of his mood shifts but at all other times he was a gifted and gentle healer. At my parents' house, family and friends were milling about and chatting. I got busy filling plates and drinks. I glanced at Alex who was talking to Oliver and at Annie and Eliza who were receiving gobs of attention from the guests. Night drew down as the guests were leaving. Alex left to go home with the girls. Mom, Oliver and I collapsed on the sofas.

During the weeks following Dad's death, my life was filled with the routine ups and downs of a growing family. My life was hopping with my kids. Alex was thriving at home and at work. Our lives were demanding. We scheduled fun and relaxation with the girls frequently to prevent burnout. Annie was energetic, exuberant and bright, Eliza quiet and contemplative. I was a mood watcher, watching moods like watching the weather, observing subtle and not so subtle shifts in mood. I was always scanning. I thought everyone watched moods, like it was normal to be constantly taking the emotional temperature of those around you. I was hypersensitive to the moods of my daughters, wondering if they might be bipolar. Sometimes, I thought everyone was bipolar.

Annie and Eliza marked time with their rapid growth and development. Annie looked like a mini-me with dark hair and brown eyes. Eliza had her father's fair hair and hazel eyes. Both girls enjoyed school, sports and a busy social life. I threw myself into maintaining the family equilibrium and liked being at the center of the family swirl. I enjoyed an extended period of tranquility never before experienced. Mom was content and busy, Oliver was settled, Alex was happy and busy and the girls were a joy. The normalcy of my life lulled me into a growing expectation of a peaceful future filled with family harmony. The only blips on my radar screen were Annie's increasingly frequent mood swings but Alex assured me that Annie's moods were normal. I allowed myself to believe Alex and started to trust the present and the future.

Our lives fell into a routine that created the core of our lives. Days blended into weeks, months and years. As time passed, my grief about my father passed. My mother had a loyal circle of friends and spent her time traveling. Oliver maintained on his medications and his work in therapy. Annie and Eliza amazed me every day as they reached for the sun, going to day care and then to elementary school. My days and nights were measured by Alex, Annie and Eliza as we separated and came together again with certainty about the stability of the orbits in our family.

Family milestones were met with regularity as Annie and Eliza progressed from elementary school to high school. Time whizzed by like a low-flying bird, unnoticed by me. Life flew by, marked with birthday and holiday celebrations. Halloweens followed by Thanksgivings at home on Beacon Hill, Christmas vacations at Alex's parents in southern California and spring vacations in Florida with Alex's sister, brother-in-law and their two kids. Annie and Eliza jumped through their developmental challenges without faltering. Alex had convinced me I had nothing to worry about in terms of their mental health as they sprouted in front of my eyes. Annie's behavior in her first year in high school started to concern me as she was staying up late, being rude and explosively angry followed by complete withdrawal into her room, giving us the silent treatment. Alex assured me her behavior was age appropriate. I worried, nevertheless.

Our Christmas visit in California with Alex's family started out as usual with a trip to the beach for a walk. We piled into Alex's mother's van and headed down to the beach. At the beach, we burst out of the van like a small explosion. Everyone talked at once. Alex's mother took charge as we stumbled after her through the sand to the shoreline and wended our way to the end of the cove. The sun was moving towards the winter horizon as we tramped back up the path to the parking area. Looking at my daughters, I wondered at their rapid growth. Our busy days and nights had cycled fast and furious at home in Boston. Visiting La Jolla slowed the speeding train down enough to assess the changes in our family. Annie had morphed into a reedy, long-haired, perky fourteen year old and Eliza, ten years old, had grown several inches in the past year.

Annie's exuberant energy was unflagging as she did cart wheels. Alex had to steady her to prevent a fall. Kate gave me a knowing glance and looked back at Annie. I had shared my concerns with Kate regarding Annie's mood swings. Kate assured me of the temporary insanity of adolescence and the guaranteed return of sanity at the beginning of young adulthood. Piling into the van, we chugged up the hill to Alex's childhood home.

"They're here."

"Who's here?" Eliza asked.

"Grandpa Tom, Aunt Kristie, Uncle Chris, Morgan and Laura. That's who's here, my dear Eliza," Kate said.

Annie was first into the house, yelling hello. Eliza hung back with me as I waited for Kate and followed her through the door to the house. Everyone talked at once as we munched on snacks and toasted with our drinks. Annie dominated the 'cousin group' as Eliza, Morgan and Laura followed her to the family room to put together a holiday play directed by

Annie. I joined them to supervise and Kristie joined us to take photos. Kristie left to help Kate prepare dinner. I stayed to help negotiate the conflicts between the director and the cast members. Annie was doing well except for her ill-concealed irritation with the cast members who at times refused to follow her directions. She became angry with me when I tried to intervene. We were summoned to dinner as Annie was accusing me of 'sabotaging' her play.

With everyone circled around the dinner table, Tom toasted the holiday season. Conversational pandemonium immediately followed his toast. After the initial burst of cheer subsided, the delicious food gained more attention and individual conversations took center stage.

"Annie, what's up with you these days?" Kristie asked.

"Oh, Aunt Kristie, you will not believe all the things I've been doing. I have three new friends. One is a boy who is so cute. I started making my own clothes. I'm on the swim team. I'm learning to play guitar. I'm going skiing with my friends when I get home. I want to start a dance club at school. I want to get my nose pierced."

As Annie continued to talk, Kate rose from the table and asked Annie to help her in the kitchen. Annie jumped up and followed her Grandmother. I gave Alex a meaningful look across the table. Annie seemed too excited to me. She was spinning too fast even for a teenager. We conversed together until Annie and Kate returned with more food and Annie once again started to dominate the conversation. She threw me angry looks when I interrupted her several times to direct attention from her to her cousins or to her sister.

After dinner, we played charades until the younger kids' bedtime. Upstairs, I helped Eliza unpack and get ready for bed.

"Why does Annie want to have her own room, Mommy? She shared this room with me last year."

"Eliza, honey, Annie loves you and thinks you're great but she' a teen now and wants to be on her own more. Teens practice being on their own, to be ready later when they grow-up. Parents help teens learn to be on their own," I said.

"Annie is crazy, Mommy. She doesn't know what she wants. She comes into my room in the middle of the night. She wakes me up and won't stop talking about her new friends. I fall back to sleep and when I wake up she's gone."

"I'm glad you're telling me this, Eliza. Annie must not wake you up at night. If she wakes you again, tell her you are going to tell me if she doesn't leave your room! If she doesn't leave right away, wake me up and I will help!"

"O.K., Mommy."

"Tomorrow, we'll go shopping for presents. At breakfast, we'll write our wish lists and pass them around. Do you remember doing that last year?"

"Yes, I remember getting everything I wanted."

The bedroom door opened and Alex slipped in onto the other bed. He had chosen a book to read to Eliza. Alex's voice was soft and soothing. I drifted into sleep lying next to Eliza.

When I woke, sunshine was coming through the bedroom window and I was alone in Eliza's bed. As I went down the hall to the bathroom, I knocked on Annie's bedroom door. The room looked as if a whirlwind had blown through. The bed and floor were covered with her clothes, books, papers and shoes. The bedclothes were strewn around on the floor. Make-up cluttered the dresser top. The mirror above the dresser was smudged with make-up like an abstract expressionist painting.

Rushing downstairs into the kitchen, I found Alex pouring coffee.

"Alex, you let me sleep with Eliza."

"Honey, you looked so comfortable sleeping next to Eliza, I couldn't bear to wake you."

"Alex, do you know where Annie is? She trashed her bedroom beyond belief. We need to talk to her and have her put the room in order."

"She's outside in the courtyard with Kristie, Eliza and her cousins."

Kristie and the kids were doing chalk drawings when Alex and I entered the courtyard.

"I hate to interrupt. Do you know where Annie is?"

"Annie went for a walk," Kristie said.

"Did she say where she was going?"

"No, she didn't."

Alex and I found Kate and Tom in the living room seated on the sofa with coffee cups in their hands. They had not seen Annie.

"We're going to look around the neighborhood for Annie. She told Kristie she was going for a walk. If she comes back in, call us!"

"Of course," Tom said. "Take my car! The keys are hanging on the hook in the kitchen by the door to the garage."

Alex and I cruised around the neighborhood in ever-widening circles. After an hour or so of driving around, we gave up and went back to the house. Four hours later, Annie had neither returned to the house nor telephoned. I was frantic. Eliza started to cry. I gave Eliza a hug and reassured her about her sister.

"Annie is practicing being on her own again, honey. We are worried about her but it will be O.K. We need to find her and we will."

"I'm calling the police," Alex said with authority, looking at me for agreement. I nodded my head in approval. Annie had never disappeared before. My greatest fear was she'd been kidnapped. As Alex picked up the telephone, Annie sauntered into the kitchen through the back door.

"Annie," Eliza screamed as she ran to grab her sister's arms.

"What's your problem, Eliza?" Annie said with disdain in her voice.

Eliza looked crestfallen and started to cry.

"Annie, I said, "Be nice to Eliza! We have all been worried about you. We have spent the last five hours waiting for you. Your father was about to report you as 'missing' to the police. Please apologize to everyone for making them worry! Come with your father and me to your room!"

"What's up with you?" Annie said to me.

I repeated my directive to Annie. "Apologize to everyone for making them worry and come to your room!"

Annie apologized and followed us upstairs. As we stood in the mess of Annie's room, I closed the door and took a few deep breaths.

Alex spoke first. "Annie, please explain the state of this room!"

"I couldn't sleep last night. I tried on all my outfits and stuff. I'll clean up."

"Yes, you will clean up."

"Annie, you know your agreement to ask permission to go out?" Alex said.

"Yes, I asked Aunt Kristie."

"You know your agreement is to tell us where you are going and when you will return. You know you have agreed to that, right?"

"Yes, but..."

"Annie, you left without asking our permission or telling anyone where you were going. You could have called us and you didn't. That is not okay," I said.

"But..."

"Where have you been?" Alex said.

Annie burst into tears as she crumpled onto the floor. Both Alex and I remained silent. Annie stopped crying, sniffled and blew her nose.

"Annie, get off the floor and sit down on the bed! Now, tell us where you have been!"

"I had to get away from here. I had to find someone my own age. You guys are driving me crazy. I didn't want to leave my friends at home and come here at all. You made me come."

"Annie, the family comes here for Christmas. When you are an adult and self-supporting, you can make decisions about where you want to be. For now, we make the rules and you follow the rules. I know you miss your friends. Where did you go?" I said.

""I went walking and I met a guy. He took me to the beach to meet his friends. We played volleyball and afterwards he drove me back here," Annie said.

Alex and I looked at each other.

"He said if I want, he'll take me out again. He says his friends get together every day at the beach. His name is Ryan and he has a dog named Pooch. He's cute and funny. His dog is cute too. He gave me his phone number."

"No, Annie, you may not call him!" Alex said.

Annie started to sputter in an unintelligible flow of disconnected words as she paced back and forth.

"Annie, look at me and listen!" I said.

I repeated my directive a few more times until Annie sat down and looked at me.

"Do I have your full attention?"

"Yes."

"How old is Ryan?"

"Umm…I don't know."

"Please tell me the rules you have broken!"

"I knew if I asked you to go, you wouldn't let me. I'm old enough to do what I want."

"No, Annie, you are not old enough to do what you want."

"Tell us the rules you broke, Annie!"

"I left without your permission. I went to the beach with someone you didn't know."

"You didn't get permission. You got into a car with a strange man. You took a big risk. You were thoughtless and irresponsible. You displayed poor judgment. There are consequences to what you have done. We're going to decide on the consequences. What do you think might be the right consequences for the rules you have broken?" I said.

"I don't think I deserve consequences. I told Aunt Kristie I was going out and all I did was hang out with some kids my age. You guys are too strict."

"Annie, let's talk more about your behavior today. Nobody always follows the rules but when somebody breaks a rule, they have to deal with consequences. In our family, we have one rule we all follow. Do you know the rule?" Alex said.

"The rule about strangers?"

"The rule about strangers is a good safety rule, to keep us safe. You didn't follow that rule. You might have been hurt by the stranger you allowed to pick you up but you weren't hurt, thankfully. I'm thinking of another rule."

"I can't think of another rule," Annie said.

"What if you came home from school and nobody was there and you didn't know where any of us were?" I asked.

"I'm getting where you two are going with this," Annie said.

"And where's that?"

"I didn't tell you guys where I was going," Annie said.

"Good thinking! What do you think might be the right consequences for not telling us where you were going?"

"Grounded, right?"

"You guessed right. You are grounded until we return home. No phone for a week, including the phone here or anywhere."

Annie nodded.

"What can you do in the future to avoid these consequences, Annie?" I asked.

"Ask permission to go out."

"Right, always ask permission to go out! Never go out without permission from us! Never go anywhere with a stranger! Never get in a car with someone you don't know!" I said.

"Annie, you knew this before you went out today. You made a decision to break the rules. You chose to ignore what you knew was wrong. For now, we want you to stay close to us so we can see you."

Annie started to cry again.

"I'm sorry. I wish I were older," she said with tears streaming down her face.

"You are fine, Annie. Let's try to work together."

Alex and I sat on either side of Annie until she stopped crying and sniffling. We marched downstairs and soon the family was bubbling with good cheer again. Later, Alex and I had a tete-a-tete alone about Annie.

"Alex, I am so worried that Annie is developing Bipolar Disorder. She's having trouble sleeping, talking too much, taking risks, and being impulsive. Emotionally, she's all over the map."

"Honey, you have just described a teen."

"I am worried."

"Let's check her diet. She may be drinking coffee or soft drinks with caffeine. Annie's pushing the boundaries and testing her independence. Molly, you are sensitized to symptoms of Bipolar Disorder, your father, your brother."

"But there are early signs during childhood and adolescence. It's occurring at earlier ages."

"Molly, it is possible that Annie has Bipolar Disorder."

"We have pulled in the reins and her response will be diagnostic. If she can't calm down and follow the rules on her own, we might need a psychiatric assessment."

"O.K., honey, let's take it one step at a time. Our girl is growing up and her adolescence is going to be tumultuous. If she has mood problems, we'll address them. Whatever happens, she's our wonderful Annie. We love her and we'll be there for her.

"You are saying all the right words, my sweet Alex."

Annie tested the limits through the next year. Alex and I kept talking to her and setting limits. As she adhered to our family's rules, she gained more independence. She started sharing her thoughts and feelings with Alex and me. She told me she 'got' what she was supposed to do. She pulled it together, getting great grades with impressive extra-curricular activities. Annie had wanted to be a doctor like her 'Daddy' since childhood. Her decision to pursue a career in the medical field resulted in her acceptance into the six-year medical program at the University of Miami. Annie's determination was unwavering once she set her mind to achieve an end.

Gathering together for Annie's high school graduation ceremony was a bittersweet event for me. Annie's time to shine and reap the harvest of her hard work had arrived. As the graduation ceremony proceeded, Alex and I were transfixed during Annie's address to her classmates, families and friends. Bursting with pride, crying from happiness and jumping for joy aptly described my response to my older daughter's graduation. When Annie's name was called and she walked to receive her diploma, our family went wild and the audience joined in. Seeing Annie's happiness and confidence gave me a thrill. As Alex, Annie, Eliza and I drove to the post graduation dinner I began to grieve Annie's imminent flight from the nest. She'd climbed the ladder out of our home and was about to be successfully launched. She'd leave for Miami in a few weeks. Her program was going to be fast and furious. If all went as planned, she would be an M.D. in six years.

Arriving at the restaurant, Alex nudged me as we walked through the parking lot.

"Earth to Molly!" Alex said.

"Let's party!" I said.

"Oh, Mom! You are so immature." Eliza said.

Annie was off to college and time started rolling faster than even before she left. Eliza whirled through high school taking a different track than her older sister. Annie loved science and sports. Eliza's interests lay in English, art, and drama and her goal was to go to Massachusetts College of Art. Eliza's high school graduation popped up three years after Annie's with the usual cast of characters in attendance plus Annie's partner, Austin, a medical school cohort. Eliza had been accepted into Mass College of Art for fall. We had a big graduation party at our place with Eliza dominating center stage. As Alex and I fell into bed at the end of the night, we congratulated each other on completing our parenting duties.

"Alex, our parenting duties will never be over. We will just be traveling more to perform them."

"You are right again, Mol! The house will seem quiet and boring without our girls. I'll make it my job to keep things exciting."

"Promises, promises," I mumbled as I fell asleep.

Eliza left for college and although she was in Boston, we did not see her often. Alex and I began adjusting to our empty nest with freedom to pursue things outside the home until my mother became ill. Mom developed a respiratory infection that wouldn't go away. I helped her every day at home until her breathing became labored and she was admitted to the hospital. The nurses were keeping visitors to a minimum, allowing me to sit with her. I read to her, helped her eat, watched television with her and dozed in a chair at the side of her bed when she was asleep.

I returned home around ten and fell asleep around eleven. At four in the morning, the telephone awakened us. Alex answered and handed the telephone to me. My mother had stopped breathing, was resuscitated and moved to the ICU. Currently, she was not breathing on her own but was on life support. Handing the telephone back to Alex, I slumped backed on the pillows.

"She's in the ICU," I told Alex.

"Oh, Molly, I'm sorry."

"I'm going to call Oliver and tell him and then go to the hospital."

"Mol, I'll go with you."

Mom was surrounded by machines with a ventilator coming out of her mouth. I stood at her bedside, stroking her hand. She was completely unresponsive. Mom and I had discussed her wishes if she were ever in need of life support. She had completed all the necessary paperwork, leaving me to make decisions for her if she became unable. She told me she did not want life support if the doctors held little hope of a recovery for her. The doctor on duty told me her infection was being treated aggressively and she might breathe on her own again.

I don't know how I made it through until morning. I stood guard by my mother's bed, holding her hand. Tears rolled in two streams down my cheeks. In the morning, a nurse persuaded me to take a break and go to the cafeteria. She assured me she would call me immediately if a change occurred. When I returned, Alex was by my mother's side. He drew me away from the bed to sit down with him. Alex had consulted with the ICU staff and had been told that my mother was not responding to treatment.

"Molly, you know the saying, 'Hope for the best but expect the worst.'"

"My father's saying was 'Where there's life, there's hope.' I know what the worst is but what could be the best. Mom told me she doesn't want life support unless she's going to recover. I know it's too soon to know if she'll recover but I don't know what to expect. Do you know if she's suffering now?"

"She's receiving medication to alleviate pain. The hope is that she is not suffering. What can I do to help you?"

"You're helping me right now? I'll call Oliver again and notify Mom's friends. I can't think of anything to do. Can you?"

"I'll call Annie and Eliza."

I reached Oliver and Mom's friends by phone and within an hour, I was in the waiting room with them.

Oliver looked terrible, big-eyed and frightened. I sat beside him and held his hand. I reviewed Mom's condition with them and asked if they wanted to visit her bedside. Oliver was silent as were Mom's friends. Her best friend, Margaret asked if she could visit her. I brought Margaret to Mom's bedside and we stood side by side in silence with the sound of the ventilator pumping away in the background. When we returned to the waiting room, another friend requested a visit. I accompanied them all one by one to stand with them by Mom's bed. Oliver was the last to visit her. He spoke to her, telling her that he loved her

Annie and Eliza arrived and had short visits with their grandmother. We congregated in the waiting room, taking turns in twos standing by Mom's bed. As I was visiting Mom's bedside with Alex, the doctor brought us to the hallway to talk.

"Unfortunately, your mother is not responding to treatment and a problem has developed with her heart. She won't be leaving the ICU in the next few days."

I was speechless. My mind refused to accept the facts as the doctor had presented them to me.

"Honey," Alex said as he leaned in to give me a hug.

"Oh, Alex," I said as I hugged him back.

I related the doctor's report to family and friends in the waiting room. As the evening progressed, people left to go home to rest. I stayed by my mother's side. Alex, Oliver, Annie and Eliza took a break to go out for dinner, bringing me back a plate of food. I ate a little and took up my vigil at my Mom's bed side. As night came, Oliver, Annie and Eliza went home to sleep. Alex and I dozed on a sofa in the waiting room. Morning came and I saw that my mother was sinking. She was immobile, pale and shrunken. I phoned Hospice and talked to their social worker. I asked her how I could figure out what direction to take now. I told her my mother would want to go home to die. She advised me to tell my mother's doctor that my mother's wish would be to go home to die. My mother's doctor told me that taking my mother off life support now would end my mother's life and advised keeping her in the ICU. I agreed to have her stay in the ICU.

When Oliver visited later in the day, I asked him to walk to the solarium with me. We sat down and looked out over Boston. I filled him in on Mom's medical status and the plan for her to stay in the ICU. I also talked about Mom's wish to be taken off life support when there was no hope. I asked him how he felt about taking her off life support if she was not recovering.

"Molly, Mom knows what she wants. She always knows what she wants. She'll let us know."

"Yes, she does always know what she wants and she will let us know, Oliver."

By the second day of Mom's being on the ICU, her condition continued to deteriorate. I didn't need the medical staff to tell me, I could see with my own eyes that she was fading away. When Mom's doctor told us there was little chance of her making a recovery, Oliver and I walked to the solarium and sat down. Before I said a word, Oliver said, "It's time, Molly, for Mom to go."

I returned to the nurse's station and told the nurse we had decided to remove Mom's life support. We said our good-byes and the machines were silenced. My mother passed from life to death. My grief was deep as I went through the motions to prepare for her cremation and memorial service. I walked through the next week in a haze with tears bursting forth at unexpected intervals. Months passed before I could make it through a day without crying when I thought of my mother. Our family had experienced the intense distress of two members suffering from major mental illness. Our coping strategies had been taxed to the max and Mom had made every effort to control the difficult events in our family as they presented themselves. She had been shaped by events, going from a vivacious, carefree young adult to a worried spouse and mother. I was happy that she had found contentment during the last years of her life. Oliver and I met at least once a week to check in and have lunch. We were both grieving less as time passed.

Life continued for the living as life always does, leaving Alex and me in our empty nest. We decided to take our next vacation to southern California to visit Alex's family. While sitting around the dinner table with Tom and Kate, Annie called to tell me she was marrying Austin in Miami at City Hall during a break from classes and their work at the hospital.

"Don't come! Austin and I made a 'to do' list and we put marriage and parenthood at the top of our list. We want to get them done soon so we can focus on our careers and get residencies at the same place. It's no big deal," Annie said.

"When are you getting married?" I asked.

"Tomorrow," Annie said.

"Okay," I said.

"I have to go, Mom. Tell Dad!"

"Congratulations, Annie!"

"Thanks," she said as she hung up.

"Alex, Annie's marrying Austin tomorrow in a civil service at Miami City Hall."

"Really?"

"Yes, really and we are not invited."

"We took our wedding vows at City Hall."

"We'll celebrate their nuptials tomorrow with champagne."

"Good plan."

Within three months, Annie and Austin were pregnant. Annie continued to maintain her 'faster than the speed of light' schedule. She was racing to the finish line. On the third day past her due date, she phoned to tell me she had agreed to take a break and stay home until the baby's birth. Two nights later, deep in sleep, I heard the telephone ring. Alex answered, as I rolled over to go back to sleep. I heard him say: "We're on our way!" Faster than lightning, I was awake, out of bed and getting our things together to fly to Miami. We rushed to the airport. On landing, we took a taxi to the hospital and dashed to the maternity floor. We rushed to Annie and Austin's birthing suite. Annie looked tired as Alex and I stood next to her at the head of the bed. Annie reached for my hand and squeezed hard.

"Annie, take a deep breath and push!" their doctor said.

"Great, let's have another push!"

"Here she is," Austin said as he caught the baby. Austin brought the baby for Annie to see and hold briefly before handing her to the nurse for clean-up and measurements. The baby, swaddled and sleepy, was brought to Annie to hold. Austin sat on the bed with Annie as they gazed lovingly at their newborn baby girl.

"Welcome, sweet Emily, welcome to our world," Annie whispered.

We each had a chance to greet and hold Emily. As I took Emily in my arms, her beauty and innocence enveloped me. Her baby blue eyes looked directly into mine. Her focus was intense and I felt the force of the bonding interaction. Time stood still as love and tenderness washed over me.

"Emily, my granddaughter," I whispered as I passed her to Alex.

As if bidden by a silent signal, we prepared to leave the new parents alone with their new baby. Following kisses, hugs and a few tears, we found ourselves in the hallway of the hospital. We set out to find a place to eat as I sang 'Happy Birthday' to Emily.

"We have a new family member," Alex said.

"She's our Emily," I said.

Later, we visited the hospital, bringing a good meal for Emily's parents' who were absorbed in their new baby. We bowed out before too long. Annie, Austin and Emily would come home tomorrow. Alex and I planned to shop for groceries, prepare meals and keep the house in order for the next few days. During the next week, Annie bounced back from childbirth quickly and adjusted to motherhood as if she had been at it for years. Their house, a comfortable ranch-style home, became a big baby nursery with baby belongings in every room. Friends and neighbors stopped by to visit and meet Emily. Annie beamed with joy.

I sensed a new bond between Annie and me.

"Mom, I finally get your intense focus on me when I was young. I did not understand why until now, with Emily instantly becoming the center of my world. It's miraculous."

As Alex and I prepared to leave Miami, I felt a new kind of heart-wrench with a special twist. I'd miss Annie as I always did but now I'd miss little Emily too. I wanted to see her every day and see all the new things she would be doing as she grew.

"Annie, Austin, I'll be coming for another visit soon. I don't want Emily to forget me."

"You are welcome anytime," Annie said. I started planning my next visit before we reached the airport.

After Emily's birth, my life took on a life of its own, speeding by like a movie being fast-forwarded. The days ran into each other like a sweet dream. I worked per diem as a hospital social worker, averaging a few days of work each week. I visited Oliver most Sunday afternoons to walk, talk and drink coffee. Oliver's life had settled into a routine of work, twelve step meetings and church. Alex and I had our routine of work, exercise, outings together and with friends. We managed to shake it up at least once a week. We visited with Eliza when it worked for her. We traveled to Miami to visit Annie, Austin and Emily when it worked for them. We kept in touch with Alex's family and visited when we could.

Eliza was whizzing through college. Six months before her graduation, she shared her plan to move to San Francisco to pursue an art career. After moving, her e-mails kept us updated on her life as she experienced the excitement of a new love relationship in the beautiful city by the bay. Alex and I traveled to San Francisco to meet Jasper as he and Eliza started a life together.

"Jasper's making dinner for us," Eliza told us as we gawked at San Francisco on the way to their apartment on a steep hill below Coit Tower.

"Everything here is bright and blue," I said as we swept up the hill, looking back at the big blue bay.

"It is beautiful day and night. The rainy season is from November to May. There's little rain the rest of the year. It won't rain at all while you're here but it may get foggy. I do love the fog," Eliza said.

Jasper had an easy-going personality. He seemed delighted to show Eliza's parents around his home town. We shared a feast with his family at an Italian restaurant and laughed again the way we had only laughed with Eliza, full of fun and abandon.

"Eliza, you have found your true home," I said as we taxied home from dinner.

"Yes, Mom, I have. I'm so glad you can see that I have found my niche with Jasper in San Francisco."

Annie, Austin and Emily had found their home in Burlington, Vermont after medical school. They were always busy on the fast track. I visited them as often as I could, Alex with me when he could get away. They visited us in Boston on their brief vacations. Unfortunately, their happy home was blown apart when Austin had a mental collapse and did not recover. He returned home to live with his family and refused contact with Annie and Emily. I stayed in Burlington with Annie and Emily until Annie adjusted to her new life as a single parent. I don't think Annie recovered from the unfortunate turn of Austin's illness. Emily consistently avoided talking about her father.

Years whizzed past without event. Eliza and Jasper decided to forgo parenthood. Annie and Emily enjoyed a peaceful life in Vermont. Alex and I were easing into thoughts of retirement with plans for new projects and travel.

"Will I have enough time?" I had picked up last minute items for Alex's birthday party. I started singing along with the music, tapping to the beat on the steering wheel. Alex was expecting to have a birthday dinner with me at home. After dinner, I'd planned a surprise party to celebrate his sixty-sixth birthday. I reviewed the entire guest list in my head. Annie and Emily were driving from Burlington. Eliza and Jasper were flying in from San Francisco. The other surprise guests included our closest friends and neighbors. I wanted to surround Alex with love, affection and good wishes as his retirement loomed.

When I arrived at home, I heard Alex singing in the shower. I had already prepared Alex's birthday dinner. The birthday cake was hidden in the refrigerator. All was ready for the celebration. I slipped into the small room at the top of the stairs and plopped down in an easy chair. Thoughts of my parents arose unbidden and streamed through my mind like phrases popping out of the dark.

I reviewed my life from the earliest memories of my father's outrageous manic behavior with his forays into sexual pursuits, outrageous shopping sprees, drunken car accidents and ceaseless talking followed inevitably by depression so deep with his irritability, his inability to get out of bed and his suicidal ideation. His steady periods when he acted normally were not as easily remembered. I dredged around my memory bank for the sweeter moments with Dad like his kind gestures towards me when he sensed I was having a hard time, his generosity when he knew I wanted something new and his uncanny way of being tuned into my moods. Memories of Mom included her efficiency, her sense of humor and her boundless energy. Mom was always the life of the party and knew how to kick up her heels. I'll never forget her dancing and laughing.

Memories of my bouts of depression clicked into focus. The mental health professionals who had cared for my father, my brother and me over the years brought hope to my heart. I often wondered what might have become of us without psychiatric care. Alex's love and care had bolstered me and continued strong. The many people I had served as a social worker gave me hope and inspiration. I recognized my experiences with my father and brother's illnesses and my bouts of depression as having enabled me to help myself and others to cope during the ups and downs of a bipolar landscape. I remembered worrying if Annie might manifest the bipolar gene. All my fears about Annie had blown away. Although my fears were ungrounded I couldn't help but wonder if the wild bipolar card would be played again.

2 ANNIE'S STORY

My mother died today. My pager had summoned me to her bedside to witness her last breath. I stood looking at her motionless body as I moved in and out of the eye of a hurricane. One moment, I was torn apart by one hundred mile an hour winds and suddenly, I became numb with a strange up and down motion. We held hands around her bed. With a great outpouring of emotion, we said our good-byes.

Last week, Mom was admitted to the hospital. Last month, I picked Mom up at her house and brought her to stay with me in Burlington to nurse her during a bout of debilitating pneumonia. Eliza and Jasper came from San Francisco. Despite intensive treatment, Mom became worse, requiring hospital care when she had difficulty breathing. Emily, Katrin and Moe came from New York. Two days ago, she became delirious, not recognizing me. Yesterday, she had started slipping away. Today, she is gone.

Two weeks ago, Mom asked me to make a promise to her to write the story of my life.

"Annie, promise me!" she said.

"I promise, Mom."

"Write it all, Annie, write the good, the bad and the ugly! You will find meaning and be set free."

Why do I need to be set free? I've adjusted to the facts of my life. I've accepted the random firing of fate, chaos, order and probability. Mom had written and shared her story with me. She often expressed how writing had helped her. Mom wanted to take care of me even after she died. She hoped I would shed the tattered remnants of heredity passed to me by her that had ripped my life apart. Life doesn't work like that, Mom. Did she make Eliza promise to write her life story? I don't want to know. I'll do as I promised.

Mom poured love like hot soup into my sister Eliza and me, watching with a hawk's eye to gauge our response. Dad's relaxed manner was easier than Mom's worried ways. Mom was wound too tight, breaking records to be the world's best mother. Dad tempered Mom's anxiety like her own personal tranquilizer. Eliza and I learned to suggest that Mom talk to Dad when she was getting herself wound up in worry. Mom's tension rolled into my life like a hurricane when I was a teen. Mom had mentioned that Grandma Molly had kept her under a microscope when she was a teen and Mom carried that storm into my life.

I sure as hell am going to miss her in spite of her hovering helicopter act. The empty air space is quiet but deadly, a black hole. Dad could make her laugh. When Dad died, she stopped laughing. When Dad's heart failed, Mom's heart broke. She gave a good performance as a grandmother, said the right things, did the right things but part of her left with Dad never to return. Now she is all gone. I can't even cry and I know I'm not making sense but I promised to write my story and I must keep my promise. I get to catalog the events that make me 'me'. 'Welcome to my world,' my mother would often say.

I was born in New York City. My parents met working in the ER. Looking at the pictures of Mom and Dad holding me when I was a baby, all bright and beautiful, smiling down at my little body, brought goose bumps to my arms and sent shivers along my neural network. They named me Annie Katherine Porter. The name was special to Mom because her best friend was named 'Annie'. Dad's mother was named Katherine. Eliza was born when I was three years old. I loved my role as 'big sister' and took the job very seriously. Mom told me her stories of being Uncle Oliver's 'big sister'. He needed a lot of care when he was sick. When Eliza was sick, I would pretend I was a doctor. I decided I would be a doctor when I grew up. Eliza and I were great buddies until we were teens. My drama queen acting-out alienated Eliza who preferred quiet, contemplative activities.

"I'm losing it, Mom," I said to the air.

"Get back to the facts," I told myself.

I summoned memories of holidays in southern California at Dad's parents' house, running down the beach with Eliza at my side, hitting the water's edge, dancing, twirling and falling down. Eliza and I would laugh so hard, we couldn't talk. Grandma and Grandpa's dogs would circle us, prancing and dancing. Mom's head would pop into view above me.

"Annie, please calm down! You're spinning too fast. Let me help you up!"

Overcome with hilarity, I reached for my Mom's hand and tried to pull her down onto the sand.

"What are you doing, Annie?" she said.

I continued pulling her down as I rolled over.

"Annie, stop! Please, stand up now!"

She pulled me up. I tried to fall again.

"Annie, stand up, now!"

I knew from the expression on Mom's face and the firmness in her tone that I was in trouble. I stood up and composed myself into a 'serious girl'. Silence prevailed, the silence born of my unspoken understanding of my mother's intense need to project calmness into chaos. Eliza may have been in danger of being swept away and drowning. Very unlikely as we were at the water's edge, far from the dreaded rip-tide currents but we were having too much fun on the fun thermostat. Mom monitored us constantly to insure we were never carried away into too much fun. She adjusted the setting of our activities to keep Eliza and me in a moderate climate at all times.

Flooded with memories, drowning in grief, I stopped writing and started to wail. I was alone in my third story attic office at home. I couldn't believe my Mom was gone. I stopped crying and watched pictures of my life rise and fall away on the screen saver of my laptop. Regaining a sense of emotional equilibrium, I closed up and went down the stairs to live my current life story.

Months zipped by like a roller coaster ride as I micro-managed my life with activities planned for every block of waking time. I had failed to include writing in my schedule but guilt arose and I pulled up my story again. I recalled wanting to be a doctor when I was a kid. Mom's father was a doctor and Dad was a doctor. I was told I would make a good doctor and I believed I would. I could not imagine being anything else. Elementary school and high school felt like an eternity until I finished and flew to Miami for my medical school program. That's when my real life began. I was exhausted most of the time but thrilled to be doing what I loved. I had a tight circle of friends, including Austin Moore who had been on my radar from the beginning of the program. His dynamic personality gave me a charge. His jet black hair and blue eyes made him hard to miss. My interest in him piqued when he alluded to his interest in psychiatry. He talked with great passion about his plan to work in a community mental health setting.

Austin and I started dating with the intensity of a tropical storm, leading to living together, getting married and having a baby. We graduated as husband and wife with our young daughter, Emily Eliza. Six years of school and training flashed by at warp speed and spit me out to the world transformed into Dr. Mommy. We moved to Burlington, Vermont for my residency in Internal Medicine and Austin's in Psychiatry. We flew from the beaches of Miami to the Green Mountains of Vermont, trading our surf boards for skis. We bought and remodeled a beautiful old house to perfection. Our little family thrived through sweet green springs and summers, brightly foliaged falls and magical white winters.

When our residencies were completed, I became a member of a group practice. Austin joined a multidisciplinary mental health team doing community services. I loved my job. Austin liked his job but complained of bureaucratic barriers to providing the best standard of care for his patients. Austin's patients were low functioning and required consistent, coordinated care to maintain their place in community settings. Mental illness, alcohol abuse, drug abuse, homelessness and non-compliance with mental health treatment were common problems among the people Austin served with his team of nurses, social workers, supportive job coaches and case managers.

His patients cycled in and out of the acute psychiatric unit. Austin and his team followed them on the unit when hospitalized, in the ER, in jail, in alcohol and drug rehab, on the streets and in their homes. The dedicated staff Austin worked alongside buoyed him up to continue to care for this group of people who could not fend for themselves but deserved the chance to attain their highest level of functioning.

Austin crashed when he lost a patient. The news of the patient's suicide headlined the front page of the newspaper. Austin's patient had jumped from a bridge onto the highway, leaving a suicide note in his room. I'll never forget Austin's discouragement during this time. One night, I came home with Emily to find him in bed in the dark. He wouldn't talk to me. I tried to engage him but he lay in bed unresponsive with a glazed look in his eyes.

I called Austin's doctor's office and she recommended an evaluation at the ER. I told Emily her Dad was sick and needed to go to the hospital. I managed to rouse Austin from bed and get him and Emily into the car. Austin slumped in the passenger seat without speaking and shuffled into the ER. Emily and I sat at his bedside until the ER doctor asked us to return to the waiting room. Austin's ER doctor called us back to inform us that Austin had been taken to the psych unit for further evaluation. I returned home with Emily, tucked her in and spent a sleepless night worrying about Austin. My life as I had known it had begun to unravel.

At the psych unit, Austin refused to see me. After several days of no response from Austin, I received a telephone call from Austin's older brother, Ben. Ben painted a new portrait of Austin. According to Ben, Austin had been sexually abused from eight to twelve years-old by a man living in their neighborhood. Austin had been warned by the perpetrator to keep the sex abuse a secret or he would kill Austin and his family. Austin eventually became courageous enough to reveal his horrifying secret to a school counselor, resulting in the arrest, trial and conviction of the perpetrator.

Ben spoke of Austin becoming a different person after the trial. Austin who had been isolated and shy became outgoing and social, devoting himself to his studies and to a new girlfriend whom he dated through high school. He talked incessantly about becoming a doctor to save lives. He ended his relationship with his girlfriend the day before he left for Miami for med school. The day he left, he told Ben he planned to marry a med student and have a family. He had little contact with his family following his departure from home.

Austin had not been forthcoming or truthful about his past with me. He related being estranged from his family due to irreconcilable differences in religious beliefs. We had been overwhelmingly busy in med school and shared little of our pasts. We were hurtling forward in the present with our eyes on the future. I wanted to get marriage and motherhood checked off my list as quickly as possible in order to devote myself to medicine. I never suspected Austin had a ticking time bomb in his brain.

To me, it seemed that Austin had cut himself off from memories of his trauma until he could no longer maintain the split. His psyche became invaded by overwhelming thoughts and feelings from his past. The final stress for him was losing a patient he knew he could have saved. Austin may have been drawn to psychiatry to heal his wounds and to help others. When stymied in his efforts to help, he may have been thrown into helplessness reminiscent of the helplessness he felt as the victim of severe sexual abuse. His defense was to withdraw completely. The explosion of his past into his life with me and Emily caused him to short-circuit. His personality had been fragmented at an early age by the sexual trauma. He had glued himself together but over time, the glue did not hold and he ripped apart. Austin chose to return to his home town with his brother at his hospital discharge.

My life transformed before my eyes. Emily was confused and depressed. She and I saw a family therapist together and Emily had her own therapist. Before his break, Austin had been the background music in the movie I projected about myself as the above-average woman achieving her potential, having it all, the career, motherhood, the husband and the home. I took no note of Austin except as he reflected my light. Granted, Austin had his secrets and his vulnerabilities which he keep hidden but I never looked below the surface of his self-created façade, never took the time to seek him out. I never blamed him as did Emily. Perhaps my accepting my failure to look honestly at Austin helped me release him and move on. Perhaps Emily blamed me for not caring for her father enough and moving on while she carried her grief in a deep pocket.

Mom moved in with me after Austin left. Dad came to stay when he could. I wondered how I might have managed without their help. Mom had been through mental health crises with her father and her brother. She knew what to say and what to do. Emily and I were in shock. Emily didn't want to talk but Mom set up art materials and Emily dove into doing lots of drawings, paintings and sculptures. Emily had always loved doing art. Emily seemed calmer after doing art with Mom. Mom tried to get me to sit down and do art work but I was unable to sit still. Throwing myself into my work helped me the most. I knew Emily was well-cared for by my Mom while I was absorbed into my work. Emily loved her Grandma Molly and Grandpa Alex. I was so grateful for their support. I cried myself to sleep every night for weeks and slowly after months, I began to see light at the end of the tunnel. Mom went home but maintained a helpful role as needed.

This writing thing is getting to me. I have had days filled with frantic work and nights of intense dreams startling me awake. I tried to hold onto the days to avoid the nights. I tried to hold onto the dreams without success. I am trying to make sense of the events in my past. I deduced that the likelihood of my choosing a mate with a mental disorder had a high probability as the tracings of mental disturbance run through my family history and mark me as a candidate to choose a mate who fit the family pattern.

Austin dropped from my life like a stone in a lake leaving endless ripples. I cannot compute the answer as to why we were rolling along on the same track with a comfortable present and a bright future when he slipped away from me. I have made several efforts to reach him but he refuses contact. His brother Ben explained that Austin is in retreat from life. Explaining Austin's absence to Emily over the years has been challenging. Sticking to the fact that her father became ill didn't cut it for her. She wanted more information. She blamed herself. She blamed me. She raged at her father with little release. She continued in therapy until she was thirteen and then jumped out like a cat on a hot tin roof.

Emily aced her life. She breezed through elementary, middle and high school piling up good grades, awards and fun times. She waltzed off to Simmons College in Boston and did well until she was nineteen when she experienced her first manic episode. A friend persuaded her to be seen at Student Health Services. From Student Health Services, she was taken to the ER. Emily called me from the ER where she had been taken for a psych evaluation. I jumped in my car and headed for Boston. Behind the wheel, I reviewed Emily's recent visit home during spring vacation. I had noted her exuberance, increased energy, self-confidence and late hours but thought she was having a great vacation. No alarms went off in my head. She had gone back to school in a flutter, looking forward to her return.

When I arrived at the ER, I found Emily pacing in a small room with a staff member. Emily stopped pacing and literally jumped into my arms.

"Mommy, Mommy, you're here."

"I'm here, Emily."

Emily started talking so fast I could not understand her. She jumped from topic to topic. She made jokes and laughed at them. She didn't seem to understand she had a problem. A psychiatric nurse joined us and explained that Emily appeared to be suffering from a manic episode of Bipolar Disorder. She did not require hospitalization but she would be unable to return to school until she stabilized on medication. We planned for her to be discharged to my care. We filled her prescriptions in Boston. She took her pills after we had dinner on the outskirts of Boston and we headed home. Upon arriving home, Emily took a sedative and went to bed. I covered her with a quilt, dimmed the light and went to bed, leaving my door open to listen for her.

The first week was difficult for both of us as Emily's mania had kicked her into high gear. As the medication began to decrease her manic symptoms, she had violent mood swings. She vacillated from shouting, wild laughing, running aimlessly and cursing to bouts of crying, tearing up paper and flinging herself down on the floor. Emily's confusion about what was happening to her consumed her attention and caused her to flail about trying to remedy her fuzzy brain. I had to give her injections prescribed by her psychiatrist in Burlington. I had arranged with my office to stay at home with her and we took long hikes in the morning and long drives in the afternoons. Emily took sedatives to sleep at night and after a week of a good sleep schedule, she began to calm down. During the second week, her mood began to normalize but she remained confused. She listened carefully to her psychiatrist's explanation about her Bipolar Disorder but she was unable to process the meaning to her on a personal level. By the third week, she was stable and made plans to return to school. The best plan was for her to return to school and resume her studies with an adjusted academic program to keep her brain active in a normal setting.

Telling my parents of Emily's bipolar break was the hardest thing I have done in my life. As a doctor, I broke bad news to people as a part of my job. Telling people bad news is not easy. Having to tell my parents that Emily had a diagnosis of Bipolar Disorder, made me sick and shook me to my core. I couldn't find the words. I was overcome with sadness and guilt. I knew my mom worried that I might have bipolar and how relieved she had been when neither Eliza nor I became mentally ill. I waited until Emily was stable and I had dropped her off at her dorm. I had arranged to have dinner with my parents at their house. I started to cry as I told them. They cried too. We talked for hours until we were exhausted. I spent the night and rose early to drive back to Vermont. To my surprise, both my parents were awake and sitting calmly at the kitchen table.

"It's going to be hard, Annie, no way it's not but Emily is resilient. She'll receive the best care. Treatment for bipolar is much better than it was for my dad and my brother," my Mom said.

"Your mom is right, honey, and you know we'll help in any way possible."

"Thanks, Dad! Emily made a good recovery from mania. She's excited to be back at school. She'll be getting treatment here. I'm hopeful."

Dad poured me a cup of coffee. As I sipped slowly, I thought of Austin's break.

"Last night, we didn't mention Austin's mental illness. I'm wondering how his illness has impacted Emily."

"I don't think it can be determined. With mental illness on both sides, the probability is higher to manifest mental illness. With early treatment and treatment compliance, Emily will have a good chance for a normal life," Dad said.

"We'll wait for Emily to tell us herself. We usually get together every month or so. I'll reach out to her soon if she doesn't contact us and invite her on a shopping trip. She loves to shop. I'll let her set the pace," Mom said.

Emily's return to college was tempered by the resources available to her on campus to receive tutoring, counseling and an adjusted academic program. Her psychiatrist in Burlington referred her to a psychiatrist in Boston. Emily's feelings about developing Bipolar Disorder were intense and difficult. She worked hard to adapt to living with mental illness. When I picked her up to come home for the summer, she was exhausted and slept most of the way home to Burlington. She complained of gaining weight, fatigue and lethargy, the side effects of her medications.

Emily and I settled into our life together at home. Emily expressed frustration with her decreased ability to manage her life as she had before her illness struck. She complained of trouble concentrating, difficulty with her memory and fatigue. Sadly, she was all too aware of the changes. This resulted in her feeling angry, frustrated, sad and confused. At least once a day, Emily would bring up her successes in high school like a tonic for her bruised ego to remember her life free of mental illness when she could do all she wished without difficulty. I cried inside every time she dug up a memory to hold to the light to look for hope. I encouraged her to believe she could achieve her goals now and in the future but she dismissed me, calling me a 'dreamer'. She hadn't had enough of normal life to be confident in herself as a young adult. She had been chopped down just as she was beginning to be a grown-up and instead of learning how to be an adult, she was faced with a major mental illness.

I walked a line of acknowledging Emily's losses and encouraging her to work to regain the abilities she could. Emily decided to take a job as a counselor at a summer camp, a job she had lined up before she became ill. Working with the kids proved to be good medicine for Emily as she was skilled at engaging the kids in the program's activities and had a gift for connecting with them. The camp supervisor complimented Emily often on her good work. Her self-confidence started to increase and she became more hopeful. Emily returned to college in the fall with renewed energy and plugged away at her work. Emily was faithful in seeing her psychiatrist in

Boston and taking her medication. She joined a psychotherapy group at the recommendation of her psychiatrist. She came home for all her vacations. Although Emily complained about her meds, about her limitations due to being bipolar and about her inability to have a 'normal' life, she worked very hard to make her life as 'normal' as possible. She changed her major from biology to psychology. She completed her course work and graduated on time with her class.

Emily had been working as a camp counselor every summer in Burlington but when she graduated from college, she found a job working with kids in Boston and moved into an apartment with friends. Emily sailed a smooth course until she decided to stop taking her medications. Her decision was unilateral and she told no one. I was unaware of my daughter's drama as it was unfolding in Boston. She became manic within six weeks of stopping her meds and became involved with a group of people who liked to party. Emily began drinking heavily and using drugs until she overdosed and was rushed to the ER by ambulance. I received a call and rushed to Boston to find Emily in a coma.

I'll never forget the night of Emily's 'undoing' as I called the event of her overdose and coma. It marked the beginning of her descent into madness. Emily disappeared into a coma for two weeks and never completely returned. Emily was discharged from the hospital to a rehabilitation facility. Emily's recovery was a slow process. She struggled to talk and walk normally and cried with each failure. Often, overcome with despair, she would lie on her bed in tears. No words of encouragement reached her. Her mood was low, despite antidepressants. I brought her gifts, books, games and puzzles to stimulate her interest. I read to her daily from novels, newspapers and non-fiction. I hung a mobile above her bed and placed photographs around her bed. I brought her quilt from home, interesting food, music, art materials and fancy new pajamas.

Emily made progress physically but emotionally she sank further and further into depression. She started to engage in self-injurious behavior, banging her head and cutting herself. My girl was sinking away. Never having been a religious person, I started to pray to the deities of all religions, to the spirits of my ancestors and to any source of healing available to help my Emily. I practiced maintaining thoughts of a positive outcome but I planned for any contingency.

My faith in medicine had never wavered until I watched my daughter slip into a vegetative state. Emily's psychiatrist recommended electroconvulsive therapy for her refractory depression. Medications had been tried with no change in her profound depression. ECT can be effective for unremitting depression when all other avenues to recovery have failed. Emily needed to consent to ECT. She was protected by law from involuntary ECT as ECT had been used inhumanely in the past.

Emily's doctor made his recommendation for ECT to Emily, reviewed the treatment in depth and addressed her questions and concerns. After she met with her doctor, Emily told me she would do anything with the hope of feeling better. "Mom, I just want to die. I don't care. If this can help, just do it!"

She started ECT. Electrodes were attached to her head. She was given a muscle relaxant and when completely relaxed, she was given a dose of electricity. She felt no discomfort other than a headache following the therapy. As her depression began to lift, she became more energetic, started talking and participating in activities. Although Emily's improvement was dramatic, she did not return to her level of functioning prior to her overdose. She spoke slowly and walked with an unsteady gait. Recovering enough to be aware of her losses, she struggled with what had happened to her. I clung to the hope of her continuing to improve as time passed.

As Emily improved, discharge was planned. I invited Emily to move home with me and she accepted. Exploring all available options for Emily's treatment after her discharge, I decided to assist her in securing mental health services in the public sector from the community mental health program in which her father had worked so many years ago. Emily qualified for public mental health services based on her diagnosis, her psychiatric history and her financial status. A week after her discharge home, Emily had her first meeting with Maddy, her community mental health program social worker. After a review of Emily' history and Emily's concerns, Maddy and Emily developed a plan for Emily. Emily was active in developing her goals in treatment. Emily complained of the side effects of her medications but she set a goal of being medication compliant. Another goal was to be clean and sober and attend twelve step meetings weekly to maintain sobriety. Maddy forged a bond with Emily, making a plan to meet with her on a regular basis.

Emily's time at home went well with quiet meals, short walks, movies at home and early bedtimes. Emily seemed relieved to be at home. Emily could no longer do all the things she could do before her overdose. I hoped she'd regain old skills and learn new skills. I planned to push her to achieve all she could but I didn't want to push her past her abilities. To sort out the effects of her overdose and the effects of the Bipolar Disorder was going to take time. The future had question marks swirling around Emily's possibilities.

Emily was engaged in her treatment and making progress in creating a life for herself. Becoming friends with people in her program, she started to meet them for lunch, dinner and special events. Months after her return home, Emily's mood shot up suddenly. Talking incessantly, prowling the house all night and dressing in outlandish outfits complete with bright make-up and odd hats signaled the onset of a manic phase. Her treatment team at community mental health quickly changed her meds and within a few weeks, the manic fire had been dampened down. Emily expressed irritation about losing the energy and excitement of the mania. I feared she might stop her prescribed medications and start drug seeking for stimulants to recapture the good feelings but she settled down and worked at her program.

Emily was determined to meet the goals she had set with her case manager. She became proficient at utilizing public transportation and prepared to apply for a job. She landed a job at a bookstore and started to save money to move into an apartment with a friend. Emily passed her probationary period at the bookstore and moved from home into an apartment. She's lived there for six months and except for minor problems like the occasional late rent check and running out of food, things have gone smoothly. Last weekend, Emily and her roommate, Josie, had a party and reported that all went well. Emily and I get together about once a week for dinner, a movie or shopping. I am worrying less and sleeping more.

Today, I have completed my promise to my mother. Having tied up my past in a tidy bundle, I release painful memories with the hope of creating happier ones. At least, I'm going to try like hell.

3 EMILY'S STORY

The party was good, everyone said so. Josie was nervous. She was worried about how she looked. I told her she looked good but she kept worrying.

"Josie, you look good," I kept telling her.

I want a party every weekend. I want a boyfriend and I could meet one at a party. I wouldn't tell anyone when I met him. Mom and Maddy will tell me not to see him. I'll go to the clubs and I'll meet a boyfriend. I had a boyfriend when I lived in Boston. We broke up when I went out with another guy and then I had that fucking overdose. Maybe I can find him again. I wonder if he's still in Boston. But I can't get to Boston, so I have to find a boyfriend in Burlington. I want a boyfriend so I can have sex again. I'm not sleepy even though it's two in the morning. I'll take a couple of extra pills and go to sleep.

Not too much sleep but I'm good to go. Dreamt Mom popped out of a closet and scared me. Mom, why did you do that?

"Hey, Emily, good morning."

"Yeah, Josie, good morning."

"How you doing, Miss Em?"

"I'm great. I have lots of ideas for how to meet a man. Want to have another party this weekend? We can invite more people this time. There are lots and lots of people I can invite. You can invite all the people you want."

"I have plans for the weekend, remember? I'm going out with Kerry and Michele. You can come."

"Josie, I want a boyfriend. Do you want to go to a club? This woman at work knows the best clubs. I'll ask her. I'll get a new outfit and shoes. Get a new haircut."

"What's up with you?"

I'm starting to get pissed off at Josie. I jump up and go take my shower. Josie can be a pain in the ass. I want to have big fun. As soon as I get to work, I'm going to ask Sara to go clubbing with me.

"Sara, you want to go dancing at the club you told me about?"

"Hey, Emily, I would but I have plans. The best place is Jupiter's Revenge. Have fun!"

"Becky, want to go dancing at Jupiter's Revenge on Saturday?"

"Saturday? I'll let you know."

I'm beginning to get pissed again but I'm not going to give up. I keep busy in the storeroom but I keep scheming on how to meet a guy when I think, 'the internet'. I leave work, rush home and get onto dating sites on my laptop. It takes hours but I get a date tomorrow night with a cute guy named Jake. We're going to meet at a place by the lake for a drink. I think I can cut down on my pills because I'm doing so good. I can be like everyone else. I've worked hard to get normal and I feel like I used to feel before Bipolar. I don't want to tell this guy or any guy that I take meds. He'll think I'm a freak. Morning pills, night pills, he'll wonder what's going on with me. And I'm going to say, "I'm crazy." No, I am not.

Mom tells me I shouldn't be ashamed or embarrassed to have Bipolar Disorder. It's like any other illness, she says. Well, I'm not giving a lecture on mental illness to a boyfriend. That would be crazy. Mom tells me my boyfriend should accept me the way I am but I don't want to tell every guy I meet. How embarrassing, 'Oh, by the way. I'm a bipolar case."

Next day, I work feverishly at my job unpacking and stocking books and more books. My boss gives me the 'good job' sign because I've done so much work. I rush to meet Jake for a drink. He looks better than his picture and we talk and drink non-stop until he takes me back to his place and we fuck until the sun starts to come up. I invite him to my place for dinner before I leave. My plan is moving forward. I have a boyfriend. I'm actualizing my life like my mother says.

Jake comes over for dinner. I've made roast chicken, veggies and rice with carrot cake for dessert. We drink a heck of a lot of wine. Before dessert, we smoke a joint, supplied by Jake. I actually don't remember too much after dessert. I wake up mid-morning when Mom calls me with Jake snoring by my side. I forgot Mom was picking me up to go to breakfast and shopping. Good thing she called to remind me. What do I do? I nudge Jake and tell him I have to go out with my mother. He can sleep some more and leave when he wants or stay but he has to stay out of sight until my Mom picks me up and we leave. He mumbles, 'fine, fine' and goes back to sleep. I throw on clothes and wait for my Mom on the porch. I wake Josie and tell her Jake's in my room and I'm going out with my Mom. 'Not cool,' she said, but I duck out before she can get going.

Mom picks me up. I know I have to tone down when I'm with Mom. I'm incredibly excited about Jake. He's the greatest guy, handsome, smart, good dresser and good in bed. I wish I could tell people but I don't trust them. They'll want to meet him and someone will tell him I have Bipolar Disorder and that will ruin it.

"What's new?" Mom asked.

"Not much. Where are we going, the usual? Let's try something new! I'm bored with the old place. There's a new place people have said is good. It's near campus. Take a right at the next light!"

Mom looked at me with question marks in her eyes so I knew I was acting too excited. I willed myself to stop talking but it was hard because my thoughts were flying at me like a bunch of frightened birds. I remembered to breathe and focus on something outside myself like the view.

"Emily, honey, you look tired. Did you sleep well?"

"Oh, I slept fine. Yesterday, I worked hard stocking a new shipment. I'm working extra-hard. I'm being given more responsibility and I can work much faster now, much faster. My boss thinks I'm great."

I knew I was talking too fast, so I stopped and focused on the view again. Now that I had things getting better, I had to keep it together so I could have a good time and not get the psych patrol to ruin it. Mom was part of the psych patrol because if she had a glimmer of my having too much fun, she would shut it down fast. She would call Maddy and my doctor. She would even put me in the hospital. She was not going to stop my fun. I've been down too long to let the good feelings go away. People don't know how nice it is to be manic. It is incredibly good. Being depressed is the pits. Being in the middle is all right but it is boring. Being manic is thrilling. Listening to music is having the notes trill along my nerves producing exquisite explosions of pleasure. Food tastes more than delicious. Sex is beyond mind-blowing, beyond bliss. Being touched by someone produces shivers of sweetness.

Manic means lots of energy, lots of good thoughts, lots of friends and lots of fun. I really would be crazy to want to give it up. Running with the fire is a state of ecstasy never to be denied. Others look at me strangely if I try to clue them into my manic world but they are askance only because they haven't been in this place of miracles where all thoughts can become reality. It's not the opposite of sad which is happy. It is good feelings to the infinite. It is your happiest moment magnified by a million. I can be a bit edgy when manic but if I get drunk, it takes the edge off. I'm able to take care of my mood by adjusting my meds and drinking when I need to slow down. Problem is I forget how much I'm drinking and blackout. Not too big a price to pay for feeling so damn good.

Days and nights are running together now with no breaks, no quiet, no sleep. Getting drunk is not slowing me. I'm cruising at high altitude with no landing in sight. Jake can't keep up with me so while he sleeps, I go out to the clubs until they shut down, then go to the all-night diner, then go home just before dawn, lie down for an hour or two and then get up and go. At work, I go too fast and make mistakes, have to go over everything and fix it but no one complains because I get so much work done. I have told Mom I have a cold and don't want to get together. I told Maddy the same story. So except for work, I'm free to do whatever I want.

Jake wants to go to the Maine coast for the weekend. He's made a reservation at a seaside hotel. He's been cooling towards me this past week but a trip will be romantic. I'm going shopping to get new outfits for the trip and a new bathing suit. Jake is a funny guy. He's always joking and making me laugh. He likes to get drunk but I can drink more than he can. He's sick the next morning and I'm not. What's up with that?

I want to quit my job and start my own business. I'll start a fashionista shop. I'll make wild outfits and sell them in my shop. I'll start small and as the money comes in, I'll expand. I'll do fashion shows and interviews. I'll advertise in big fashion magazines. Maybe I'll move to New York, the fashion center of the world. I'll start working now since I don't need to sleep. I'll use my clothes to make new clothes. I'll set up my sewing machine in the kitchen and get to work. I'll listen to music while I work and make some great outfits. I'm feeling edgy. I'll have a beer. I'll cut up the red shirt and the lavender shirt and make a crazy quilt kind of thing. Strips and rectangles over-lapping, put some plastic on top, add irregular buttons by painting the buttons, paint the shirt too.

"Emily, what are you doing?" Josie said.

"I'm making an outfit."

"Do you know what time it is?"

"Around two."

"Right, two in the morning. You woke me. You're making too much noise."

"All right, I'll move into my room."

"Emily, keep it quiet!"

I worked in my room and made three bright and beautiful shirts. I was starting a fourth one when the sky started lightening up. I continued making outfits. I worked until I ran out of material. I took a trip to the fabric store and got more material. Good thing Mom gave me a credit card. She made rules about how to use it but she'll be happy when she sees what I've done and hears my plan for being a fashionista. I'm going to make her so proud of me. She can come to my grand opening. I can make an outfit for her. I'll use her favorite colors and textures. This is going to be so good. I kept at my fashion work until it was time to get ready to go to Maine with Jake. I packed a couple of bags so I'd have enough stuff to make choices. I like to have lots of choices in everything but especially outfits. I had three bathing suits, one for each day we'd be there.

Jake looked surprised at all my sewing stuff strewn around my room but grabbed my bags and we hit the road, getting to our hotel on the coast around ten. The room was beautiful with a view of the ocean. We swam in the pool and played around. I could hardly stop laughing. We had sex in the big bed. I was wide awake when Jake fell asleep so I went down to the bar for a drink. That's where the trouble started. A guy named Brad bought me drinks. We talked about lots of different things. I woke up in the morning with Brad curled around me in his room. I started to get worried. My clothes were on the floor beside the bed. I dressed and slipped out of the room.

Unfortunately, Jake was awake when I opened the door to the room. When I told him I didn't remember how I got to this other guy's room, he blew up at me. He stuffed his things in his bag and left, saying. "Let this other guy take you home!" He walked out and slammed the door. I took a shower, dressed and headed for the dining room. After eating, I donned my bathing suit and went to the pool. Brad joined me poolside and we started drinking and talking. When he took off without inviting me to come along, I stayed at the pool. When I got bored, I put on my shift and sandals and went into the bar. A guy named Eric joined me. We shared drinks and a meal. We talked and laughed as if we had been friends forever. I invited Eric back to my room.

We were messing around on the bed, when Eric started getting rough and hurting me. I backed off.

"What's your problem, Emily? You seem like a free spirit who would enjoy a little more action. Come on!"

I don't like pain, I like pleasure."

"There's a fine line between," Eric said.

"Don't cross the line!"

He grabbed me and started hurting me. I yelled at him to stop but he didn't. He was really hurting me now, thrusting hard, slapping and biting. He put his hand over my mouth and became vicious. The pain was excruciating. I was in agony and had trouble breathing. As he continued for an interminably long time, I started to panic, thinking I might die. When he finally stopped and got off me, I could barely move. My nose and mouth were bleeding and I felt like my lower body had been attacked with knives inside and out. I held my breath as I watched him put on his clothes and leave the room. I got up and put the safety lock on the door. I took a hot shower, got dressed and went to the bar. I didn't want to talk to anyone. I sat at a secluded table in the shadows and ordered drink after drink.

I woke up in a hospital. A nurse told me I had been brought to the ER by the police who had been called to my hotel when I passed out in the bar and could not be revived. I gave a report of my rape to a police officer. I talked to a rape counselor. I called Mom and told her what had happened. She came and stayed with me until I was discharged. She brought me to her house. The ER doctor had given me sedatives for sleep. I took two and went to sleep.

Mom tells me I slept for twenty hours. I'm groggy but coffee should kick-start me. Mom's not saying much but she's looking her worried look at me. I've learned her expressions well. I'm worried she might try to put me in the psych hospital but I have learned no one can make me take meds if I don't want meds and no one can lock me in the hospital unless I'm a danger to myself or to others which I am not and can prove it. I have to get back to my apartment to work on my fashion pieces. I have images of pieces I want to make, passing on runway models. Caffeine is zinging me up and I want to get moving.

"Hey, Mom, good breakfast. I love your cooking."

"Stay here for a few days and I'll make your favorite foods. Let's take a few days off from work and we'll have mother-daughter time."

"Um, actually, I'm working on a fashion project at my apartment and want to get over there. Can you drive me?"

"Emily, you need to take it easy. Your project can wait."

"No, Mom, I want to get back to it now."

"All right, I'll drive you to your apartment."

Mom walks out of the kitchen. I clean up and gulp another cup of coffee. Mom takes her time getting her stuff together to leave. I am irritated and feel like screaming at her but pace around waiting for her. I don't want her to know how excited I am. She can't do anything to stop me but she might try. She could start talking her 'doctor talk' if I don't calm down. A drink would help calm me down but she'll have a fit. I pop one of the sedative pills from the doctor at the ER and go outside to wait by her car. Finally, Mom comes out and slowly walks to the car.

"Emily, you seem restless."

"I'm fine, Mom. I have a lot to do today. I just want to get going. Can we go, please?"

"Em, do you think you are manic?"

"Mom, come on, can I just feel good without you asking me if I'm manic?"

"But, Emily I would not feel good if I had been raped."

"Well, Mom, I'm not you. I was raped but I want to move on and keep busy."

"All right, Emily."

We rode in silence, hard for me to not talk but I had to stay still to get to my place. My thoughts were colliding but I was able to keep my mouth shut. Mom pulled into the gas station, jumped out to fill the tank. I was sweating so I jumped out of the car, walked into the store and bought a pack of gum. Back in the car, Mom drove past the turn to my apartment.

"Mom, you missed the turn."

"I'm going to do a few errands, the bakery and the cheese shop. We can get what you want for your place."

"Mom," I said, trying to modulate my voice, "I have everything I need at home already. I want to go home now."

"Emily, let's spend a little more time together. I'm beginning to think you don't want to be with your old mother."

"It's not that. I told you, I have work to do. Please, take me to my place!"

"Okay, I'll take you now."

"Mom, you are treating me like a child. I'm an adult and I'm going to work hard and make it big with my fashions. I've already wasted time and I want to start working."

"Tell me about your fashions!"

"I'm making a new look. Unique fabrics quilted and appliquéd with unusual attachments, in shirts, jackets, pants, dresses, skirts and bags, combining old-fashioned quilting with high-tech materials to create a fashion look of the past blasting into the future."

"How will you market your work?"

"Get a shop on the lake and then take my show to New York and Los Angeles. Will you co-sign for a business loan for me?"

"Emily, slow down! Show me what you're doing!"

"I'll e-mail you photos of what I've done so far."

Finally, we pull up to my apartment building.

"Bye, Mom," I said as I jumped out and ran up the path to my place.

Finishing a dress of purple velvet and yellow silk with a lavender wood print, I take a break to eat. I had been alternating wine and coffee to keep me calmly energetic. I am as hungry as a bear. I ransack the kitchen, throw together leftovers, turn on the TV and eat. As I'm cleaning up, Josie comes in.

"Hey, Josie, how are you?"

"Fine. How was your trip to Maine?

"Oh, pretty good. I'm done with Jake. Time to move on. No big deal. Want to go out tonight?"

"No, I have to work tomorrow."

"I'm going, might be quiet on Sunday night but I'll check it out."

The club is not jumping but it is not empty either. It isn't belly up to the bar but people are dancing and drinking. I sit at the bar and order a drink. A guy asks me to dance. We sit down at a table, talk and drink. I remember having quite a few drinks. I wake up in the alley behind the club lying on top of a pile of trash. The sky is getting light. I stand up and wobble around. I have no clue what has happened to me. I feel wretched all over but I'm not bleeding or broken anywhere. I walk home and slip into my room. I stuff my fashion designs and my stuff into a big suitcase and wait for Josie to leave for work. When I hear her leave, I call a taxi and hop a train to New York. Emerging into the station in New York, I'm entranced with all the rushing people. I'm on my journey to fame. I can feel it in my bones. Why have I listened to people who cautioned me to stay on meds and not stop? I am done with taking orders from anyone. I check into a dive of a hotel, dump my stuff and start to explore the city. I scope out places to bring my fashion designs. I'm on my way to fame and riches. I have a hot dog from a street vendor. I wander through Times Square as dark descends. I have visions of my fashions flashing across the huge light displays above Times Square. I prowl around looking for a drink and go into a pub, settling into a booth. Two cute guys ask if they can join me. The guy sitting next to me starts buying my drinks. The other guy invites a woman at the bar to join us. We have fun flirting, joking, laughing and drinking.

Next thing, I wake up in a bed in a room with tiled walls and bars across the window. I'm in a hospital gown. I keep trying to slam the brakes on my brain but I'm going full steam ahead with words and thoughts blurring into each other as they rush like a torrent in a swollen, flooded river. I feel like I have hospital drugs on board. The torrent freezes mid-stream and my mind goes dark and then without warning the thoughts, words, images attack me again like an inflamed crazed colony of bumblebees. When I try to get out of the room, the door is locked. After I pound on the door, a woman unlocks the door and helps me get cleaned up. She takes me across the hall to an interview room and leaves. Eventually, a man comes in and sits down.

"Hi, I'm Jerry Reynolds, psychiatric nurse. Do you know where you are?"

"No. Where am I?"

"You're at Psychiatric Emergency Services. Do you remember how you got here?"

"I remember being with some people at a pub."

"According to the police officers who brought you here for evaluation, you assaulted a man with broken glass and cut his face. He needed stitches."

"No, I didn't do it."

"There are several witnesses to the assault. According to the victim, you screamed at him that you are bipolar and he should leave you alone. Do you have Bipolar Disorder?"

"Yes, but I didn't hurt anyone."

"What is your name?"

"Emily Moore. I need to get out of here."

"Emily, you are legally detained for a psych evaluation."

"No, you are kidding me. I've never hurt anyone in my life. You are wrong, wrong, wrong!"

"Emily, I'm telling you the truth. Did you drink alcohol and use drugs yesterday?"

"I had some drinks, no drugs. At least I don't remember drugs."

"Are you taking any medications?"

"No, no meds lately."

"What meds have you taken in the past?"

"Lithium and others, lots of others I can't remember."

"Where do you live?"

"I just got here. My stuff is at a hotel."

"Where were you living before you came here?"

"Vermont, Burlington."

"Do you have a job?"

"No, I'm pitching my stuff to work as a fashion designer."

"How often do you drink and use drugs?"

"I drink every day and drugs not too much."

"Emily, how would you describe your mood lately?"

"I've been happy, busy, having fun."

"How much have you been sleeping?"

"Not much. I have too much to do."

"Have you had racing thoughts?"

"Oh, yes, fast thinking."

"Have you been hearing voices or seeing things that aren't there?"
"No."

Any thoughts of hurting yourself?"
"No."

"Any thought of hurting anyone else?"

"No. I told you I've never hurt anyone."

"Where are your parents?"

"My mother is a doctor, lives in Burlington, Vermont. My father left us when I was a kid. I don't remember him."

"Do you know of any mental illness in your family?"

"Oh, yes, my father was crazy, my mom's father and brother were crazy."

"Do you know the names of their mental illness?"

"My father, I'm not sure, Grandpa was bipolar and my uncle too, bipolar. Pretty messed up, right?"

"Do you have contact with your family members?"

"I am sick of my mom interfering in my life. I don't want to see her anymore. I don't want to see anybody in my family. I'm going to take care of myself and do what I want to do."

"When did you have your first bipolar episode?"

"In college."

"Have you been depressed?"

"Yes."

"Have you attempted to kill yourself?"

"I've thought about killing myself but never tried."

"Have you been manic before?"

"Oh, yes, I have and I want to be manic all the time."

"Emily, you seem to get into trouble when you're manic like drinking, getting into fights and coming to the emergency room. What do you think about the trouble you get into when you are manic?"

"I think you're crazy. I'm doing great. You wish you could have as much fun as me. Maybe we could have sex and I can show you how great manic can be."

"No, Emily. Have you been having sex more than usual?"

"You bet. When I started feeling better, I started having sex, first with Jake then another guy."

"Emily, I know you said you don't want contact with your mother. It might help you to talk to her."

"Oh, no, she'd be here quicker than the speed of light, scoop me up and take me to her house and make me her prisoner again. She doesn't want me to have fun. She'll drive so fast she might crash. Her car is pretty speedy."

"Emily, let's go over a few things. You are here because you injured a person seriously. You were brought here by the police because you have a mental illness but you will face charges for assault. Do you understand?"

"Yes."

"Our doctor is going to meet with you soon."

Eventually, a chubby man with brown curly hair came in and introduced himself as Dr. Herran. He asked me a bunch of the same questions Jerry had asked me. I answered all his questions and he left the room. Jerry came back to tell me that for my safety and the safety of others, I was to be transferred to the psychiatric unit. I became so irritated I started screaming. Three people came in and asked me to calm down. When I didn't stop, they tied me down and gave me a shot in the butt.

My first clear thought on the psych unit was the day Mavis came to visit me.

"Hello, Emily, I'm Mavis. I'd like to talk to you about your upcoming court date. Do you want to talk to me?"

"Sure."

"I work for the Department of Mental Health with the Forensic Mental Health Team," Mavis said as she handed me her card. I read her card and looked up.

"Hi, Mavis, what's with the court date?"

"Good question, I can help you with your court date by arranging legal assistance and offering the court a way to keep you from jail time for your offense. Are you interested in hearing more?"

"I am."

"Okay, well, I can introduce you to a lawyer who will go to court with you and present a plan to the judge to consider. The plan will be for you to agree to receive mental health services from the Department of Mental Health. Any questions now, before I tell you what the plan for your mental health services will be, if you accept?"

"Tell me what I'll have to do!"

"I'll tell you. You would have to sign an agreement to follow a plan that will include monthly visits to our psychiatrist, to take the medications the psychiatrist prescribes for you without any significant break and to meet with me or another case co-coordinator as frequently as needed. A case co-coordinator assists you with psychiatric doctor appointments, getting your medications, staying on your medications, housing and medical needs. There may be a few other conditions ordered by the court. What do you think of the plan?"

"Sounds okay. I've had a case worker before, in Vermont."

"How did that work for you?"

"Pretty good but I would hide a lot from her."

"Hiding things from people can cause problems like having to be in the hospital. Mental health services can help you stay out of the hospital and out of jail."

"I don't want to go to jail. I'm in jail here and I want out."

"I have to tell you, Emily, the lawyer will tell you too, that you can plead 'not guilty' to your charges but there is a victim, the guy you assaulted, who is planning to testify against you. But I want to tell you that in my experience, most people who have a mental health diagnosis and commit a crime, are more likely to avoid jail time, if they plead 'no contest' with a written plan of the mental health services that they have agreed to follow. It's better if they have started working with the mental health department before their court date. You can start now, if you wish. Any questions?"

"So, you're telling me I might go to jail even though I don't remember what I did?"

"Yes, Emily, there is a strong possibility you may go to jail but a lawyer can answer your legal questions better than I can. I can arrange a meeting with a lawyer to get your questions answered. You can decide about whether you want mental health services after you talk to a lawyer or you can sign on now for mental health services. It's your decision. You're free to accept or reject mental health services at any time. You are not free to skip your court appearance. If you do skip your court appearance, an order will be issued for your arrest."

Mavis paused. She and I sat in silence. Mavis opened her bag and pulled out a sheaf of papers. She pulled out a paper and handed it to me.

"Emily, this describes what I've been telling you. One other thing I have to tell you is that even if you decide to sign on for mental health services, the judge may sentence you to jail time. I think a lawyer will tell you that you have a good chance of getting deferred to forensic mental health because this is your first offense but there is always a chance you will get jail time. If you get deferred from jail on probation with mental health services, you will be required to follow your mental health plan. If you do get jail time, you can receive mental health services in jail. Take your time and read it and then I'll answer any questions you have."

As I read, Mavis started writing on her pile of papers. As I read, I understood my choices were limited. Accept mental health services or risk going to jail. I had better opt for the 'get out of jail free' card. I might be crazy but I'm not stupid.

"Okay, Mavis, I'd like to sign up for your service today, right now, please."

It became evident that I had made the right decision to sign up with Mavis. I met with an attorney on the unit who prepared everything. I signed gobs of papers, agreeing to whatever I had to agree to in order to be set free. I took my meds, started calming down even though I wanted to hold onto the high. My attorney presented everything in court and I walked out a free woman. Mavis put me in temporary housing and within weeks, I had my own little apartment. I was given probation. If I missed my mental health appointments or stopped taking my meds, I'd go straight to jail. After a few months, I was feeling better. I missed the high but I didn't miss the fallout from the stupid things I did when I was high. I was terrified of falling into depression's grip like the darkness was stalking me but Mavis helped me deal one day at a time. I made friends, got back to work on designing fashions and kept clean and sober.

One fall afternoon, a light tap on the door of my tiny apartment grabbed my attention from the tangle of fabric I was wrestling. My place was covered with outfits, fabric, decorations, thread, ribbon, trim and junk. My sewing area was littered with half-finished pieces. I ignored the tapping on my door.

"Emily, it's Mavis. Please answer the door! I have good news for you."

Mavis is my miracle worker. Since our meeting, she has helped me to stay out of jail and to navigate into a safe place where I can do my work. She helped me find a place to live when I was discharged from the psych unit and has given me good advice without being stuck-up about it. I run to let her in.

"Emily, I was able to get you a referral to an agency to help you market your fashions. You have to call to set up an appointment for a meeting. I told you life would work better if you stayed on your meds."

"That's great, Mavis. Thanks so much. I can't believe it. Meds do help me stick with it, instead of making and then losing it. I don't have as much energy or inspiration but I am getting it done."

"You are welcome. Here's the phone number to call for the appointment. Want me to stay while you call?"

"Sure."

Mavis was keeping me on the path and helping me to get a show for my fashion designs. She believed in my talent. Mavis says you need connections to get a start in the fashion world. She's a social worker with connections. I met with Jon Hewitt, Mavis' connection and he gave me the break I needed. He looked at my portfolio, made phone calls and within two weeks, I was scheduled to show five pieces at the "Bright and Beautiful" fashion show, a show for up and coming designers. Excitement fueled my work as I increased my output, paying special attention to my mental health maintenance program. My awareness of Bipolar Disorder and how to avoid the pitfalls has increased. I can no longer deny I have Bipolar Disorder and I accept that I must have treatment. At times, I become discouraged and wonder, "Why me?" but Mavis reminds me to look on the bright side and I do.

I worked like a maniac up until the moment my models were ready to walk down the runway. As they launched forward and were greeted with wild applause, I gave myself to laughter and to tears. If nothing else happened, I knew I'd be happy forever, for my dream had come true. At the reception following the show, I was surprised to see my mother walking towards me.

"Emily, congratulations!"

"Mom, you're here. What a surprise!""

"I saw an announcement for the show with your name listed in The New York Sunday Times. Your work is fantastic. Hope you don't mind that I came."

"I'm glad you're here as long as you don't try to take me away."

"No, I will not take you away. I wish I had been supportive of your talent in fashion. I apologize for being too focused on your symptoms. If I'd had a more positive focus, I might have helped you. I hope you can forgive me."

"Thanks, Mom. Of course, I forgive you. I tried to hide everything from you. I hope you can forgive me."

"Emily, I forgive you. I'm staying in New York for a few more days. I hope you and I can get together for a shopping adventure and dinner."

"Sure, let's do it tomorrow!"

"Great. Want to meet me at my hotel around two?"

"Sounds good!"

On our shopping adventure the next day, Mom asked for 'Emily Moore Designs' in every store we shopped. At dinner, we talked and laughed like old friends. She was loving and supportive with no demands, no conditions.

"I'm so proud of you, Emily."

"Thanks. Sorry I left Burlington without telling you but I wanted to do it on my own."

"You did the right thing. I know it was hard but you found your way."

"Maybe I'll visit you in Vermont some day but I'm not ready to do it yet."

"Emily, I understand. Whenever you are ready to visit home, home is there. In the meantime, let's have more shopping sprees here in New York. Call me and I'll come."

"Deal, Mom, deal."

After the many trips into bipolar spins that had ripped my life to shreds, I stuck to my mental health treatment plan with the help of Mavis and climbed the ladder to make my fashion house a success. Driven to design innovative fashions, I worked tirelessly to keep doing what I knew I was supposed to do. I hired the right people to create and run my business, I created the right contacts, I pushed to have fashion show after fashion show and I lucked out with good reviews and hoards of people buying my stuff. I functioned well in the high stress of the fashion world because it suited my mood swings. With each swing through a well-medicated mania, I created my designs with astounding speed and grace. My well-medicated dip down was a fallow period in which I monitored production. On my upswing, I would be ready for the fashion shows, the meetings with the media and the public and the promotion of my business. If my mood cycles didn't correspond to the fashion cycles, I had brilliant and skilled employees who shared my vision and kept things running well if I faltered.

On the roller coaster of my life, I met Mark, an investment broker at a fashion extravaganza benefit. We were chatting when my designs were modeled and auctioned. When I mentioned I was seeking investors for my company, Mark picked up the ball and ran with it. We met for dinner a week later. After the business talk, we flirted shamelessly and before long, we were a steady item. Mark and I spiraled through marriage, through a pregnancy with me off all my meds and through a separation and divorce because he could not handle my mood swings when I was pregnant and unmedicated.

Mom helped me hire a great divorce lawyer to protect me, my unborn child and my business. Moe was born with my mother as my birth coach. Mom hung in for me without a word of advice or criticism. She had my back when I crashed into a nasty post-partum depression, moving into my apartment with Moe and me until my meds kicked in and I had recovered enough to take on motherhood and my career. Mark turned out to be as feckless as my father, cutting off all contact with me and Moe. My business was maintained by my brilliant staff while I was sick. I pulled out of depression in time to do the designs for the spring show. Back on meds, I took the helm of Emily Moore Designs and made it happen.

Good fortune shined on me as my business expanded with my staff doing outstanding work and allowing me to do my thing in the art studio. We hired talented designers to fill up our offices as we continued to top the fashion bests and reap profits. My business manager, Jenna, and my publicist, Andrea knew how and when to take over and protect me and the business through all the permutations of my moods. During my super-charged bursts, I create my designs, putting together an enormous collection. I become feverish, combining and subtracting color, line, form and whimsy until each piece is runway ready. My work schedule is erratic and beyond my control. I create when the fire is burning and I smolder the rest of the time. I'm always sketching, drawing, designing but nothing zings into total originality until my brain produces the magic formula. Then, I don't eat, I don't sleep and I don't leave my studio until I experience a sense of completion, satisfaction and contentment.

Motherhood has slowed me down but Moe has an area in my studio where he can sleep and play. I hired Terry, a graduate student who tends him while I work. She studies while he's sleeping. She's become part of the family. I love taking breaks to play with my little Moe. Moe doesn't seem to mind that I'm bipolar, he loves me totally. I can do no wrong in his baby blue eyes. When my bipolar brain is messing me up, I have a back-up team in place. Mom told me I can call her anytime, she'll hop the train and head to New York to help me. Like I said, lady luck is on my side.

I want the world to know that Emily Moore, former mental hospital patient, is alive and well in New York City with plans cemented for her fashion house backed by big-time investors. Little Moe is growing from a little baby into a little boy. I have never been this happy without being manic. I've been sticking to my medication and therapy appointments as I have learned my lesson. "No meds, no nothing!" My social worker kept telling me that I was my own worst enemy and I thought she was crazy, not me. The truth of her words has manifested and I listen closely to her words of wisdom. Mavis believed in my talent. My mom believes in my talent. I'm surrounding myself with staff that believes in my talent and has the skills to make my vision a reality.

Suddenly, with my new-found fame, I have heard from my ex-husband and my father, of all people in this wide world. They both accused me of being 'too crazy' and walked out of my life. I realize I was hard to take off meds but they threw out the baby with the bathwater. It's a metaphor for them not seeing the good, strong parts of me, only seeing the bipolar parts of me. My mom hung in with me through the thick and thin of my manic-depression and even she dismissed my abilities to create new and exciting designs. Mom gets a pass because I know she loves me and has my back, always has but my ex and my father can go to hell. They are not cashing in on my fame, no way. They have made their own headlines on my fame as I have emerged into the spotlight. When the press tracked my father down, he agreed to an interview. Can you believe it? After dropping into a black hole when I was a little girl, he's well enough to talk to the media. I can't wait to hear what he has to say. When the press asks me, I'll tell them my father abandoned me. I don't know him and don't want to know him. My ex is a joke although he did help me get my start. I guess he deserves a little of the spotlight. He abandoned Moe.

Grandma Molly would tell me I could do anything I set my mind to do. She got it when I went all bipolar. She really did. She told me she had mood swings and took medicine. She said she wouldn't have made it without meds and therapy. She told me about my great Grandpa and my Great Uncle having bipolar. Grandma Molly told me a lot. She told me I was creative and artistic when I was little. She would do art stuff with me for hours. She still has all my art stuff. Moe does art with her now.

"Where's my Moe? Where is he hiding?" I said as I swept into our apartment. My apartment is worlds nicer than the closet I lived in when I first came to New York. I have gobs of space and have hired really cool people to help me out.

"Here's my boy! What have you been doing, Moe? Have you been playing with your trains? Let's play, Moe!"

As the spring fashion blitz winds down and the dog days of summer heat the streets of New York, Mom proposes spending the summer in the Hamptons on Long Island. I jump at the chance to get Moe out of the city. I know a few people who summer in the Hamptons and soon, I'm off to dinners and parties in the evening with Mom watching Moe. I can sense her apprehension about my going social but she doesn't say a work. I tell her about all the parties I've been attending in the city and my absolute commitment to my mental health program.

My vacation with Moe and my mother falls into days on the beach and evenings at home or with friends. Jude, one of my best friends from the fashion biz, has invited me to his regular Friday night gatherings. He introduces me to Katrin and within a moment, I fall in love. As I watch Katrin, I think I must be getting crazy again for I have never fallen in love like this. I don't trust my feelings but I am drawn to her and invite her to visit me and go to the beach the next day. I am able to sleep well, so I don't worry about mood slippage because the first sign of mood trouble for me is trouble with sleep, either too much or too little. I have a whole crew in the wings, waiting to swoop in and help me if I get sick so I am ready to take the plunge with Katrin.

Katrin and I discover a world of commonality as we get to know each other. Having moved to New York from England, Katrin is a fashion photographer. We spend hours talking and laughing, comparing our experiences and our acquaintances. Katrin tells me she's a lesbian and I tell her I'm bipolar. Before long, we make love on the beach under the moon. Katrin comes home to my house to sleep and we are together from that day forward. My mother welcomes Katrin into our family circle and Moe goes bananas over her. I tell Katrin the stories of my bipolar blow-outs as she holds me tenderly.

"Emily, I love you and I'm with you no matter what happens."

"You say that now but if I go off my meds, you may see things differently."

"We don't know, do we? I want to be with you. I know that."

"Katrin, Katrin, Katrin…"

Back in the city in September, we become the hot news for about a week and then fade into the background. I'm in my usual fall funk and worry that Katrin will pull away but she stays her steady self and hangs out in bed with me. The three of us, Katrin, Moe and me pile up in the living room and in the bedroom for long naps and playtime. Katrin moves in a few weeks before Christmas and we usher in a truly happy new year. Spring sees me perking up and doing my job in the studio. It was a busy time for Katrin, too, but we eked out time for us and time for Moe. Mom came to visit us and to be with Moe who was crawling and babbling. I was beginning to feel normal like a person without mental illness. To think in that vein was dangerous for my treacherous mind led me down the path to thinking I did not need meds. I was deluded enough to think I was well enough to be off meds because I had a happy home life. I sank into the deepest depression in my life.

Sweat covers me like a cold damp blanket when I wake up in a hospital bed with an IV in my arm. Light streams through the window blinding me. Panic runs through me like a race horse. As I'm gasping and blinking, a nurse named Holly comes in and stands at my bedside. She helps me to the bathroom and back to the bed. I notice a woman sleeping in the bed on the bathroom side of the room as I toddle on Holly's arm back to my bed between the window and the pulled curtain.

"How did I get here?"

"Emily, I'm your nurse, Holly. You are at the Heights Hospital. You were brought in by ambulance. Your roommate called 911 when she found you on the kitchen floor unconscious and having seizures. Your stomach was emptied of a drug overdose in the ER and you were admitted. How do you feel?"

"Bad," I said.

I did remember weeks of lying in bed crying. I remembered sleepless nights lying on the sofa in the back room or lying in bed next to sleeping Katrin. My mind is fogged with intermittent glimpses of scenes with different people moving about and talking. I remember Katrin and my mother asking me to see a psychiatrist. I remember thinking I should die.

A food tray arrives and a woman named Kim sets me up to eat. I have no appetite. I am thirsty, pick up orange juice, poke a hole through the carton with a straw and take a few sips until the juice hits my stomach and grabs too tight. I push the tray table away and close my eyes. I am enveloped in despair.

A woman in a white lab coat comes to my bedside.

"Hello, Emily. I'm Dr. Patel, hospital staff psychiatrist. May I sit down and talk with you, please?"

"Hi, yes, please sit down."

I tell her my bipolar history and my family's bipolar history. I tell her the meds I've taken and my decision to quit meds. I start crying and can't stop.

"Emily, Emily, let's try to work together to get this better for you!"

We talked together about my being depressed like I had a cold or something, no big deal. Meds would help me. I signed consent for treatment and informed consent to take an anti-depressant and a mood stabilizer. After Dr. Patel leaves promising to visit me next morning, I call Katrin.

"Katrin, I'm so sorry. I couldn't see any way out of my depression."

"Emily, I wish you had told me. I knew you were in a battle with depression but I didn't think you were suicidal. Your mother is on her way. When she gets here, I'll set her up with Moe and come to see you."

"Moe, how is Moe?" I said as the tears start streaming again.

"Moe looked for you and said your name, 'Meme' like he does but when I told him you were out, he pointed to the front door. When I said 'yes', he started playing."

"I'm letting you guys down, I'm so sorry."

"Emily, don't even think like that now. Like you've told me, your brain is not your friend when you are sick. You are suffering from an illness, depression, and your brain lacks the chemicals you need to function. Give yourself time, take the medication and come home to me and Moe."

"Thanks, Katrin. See you when you get here. Bye."

Swimming up from the dark, light shatters into colors as I wake in the hospital again. Dr. Patel stops by and tells me I'm medically cleared and will be moved to the psych unit today. When I ask her when I can go home, she tells me in a few days. After my transfer, I rest in my room, sleeping, eating and making attempts to read. Katrin and my mother take turns visiting me. I want to go home but I know I have to follow protocol to get out. The next day, when the unit psychiatrist asks me if I am having suicidal thoughts, I tell her that I am not. Wisps of suicidal messages still float through my consciousness but I remember that my brain is not my friend and tell the thoughts to go away. My brain is tired but I can feel depression starting to trickle away in a tiny rivulet. Katrin told me she understands that I was sick when I took the overdose. I leave wreckage behind me like a hurricane when I'm sick and I'm embarrassed after I've made a stupid move like this one.

My 'retreat' was well handled by my staff. According to them, Emily Moore had never left the building but had continuously reigned supreme over her fashion empire. They kept my star burning brightly as I lay in bed day after day unable to get up, waiting for the antidepressants to take effect. Every night, I lay in bed with tears dripping into my pillow, wondering what had happened to my other self, my happy, vibrant, successful self who could speak in a clever way, charm people, have fun and dance all night. I went off my meds and created a big 'glitch' and I have paid a price. I hope my relationship with Katrin is okay. I have learned that life on the shifting sands of mood disturbance requires constant adjustment. Loving me through my mood swings requires fortitude, compassion and patience on the part of Katrin. Katrin has hung with me through my ups and downs so far but this time I went way down. I hope I didn't go too far.

Fortunately, the psychotropic drugs have worked again and I am being restored to homeostasis. My lift off from depression is well underway. One might say a miracle has transpired, transforming Emily from a bedridden invalid whose mind was riddled with suicidal thoughts to Emily today, active and looking forward to life. I have gone from having seizures on the kitchen floor caused by an overdose with the intent of ending my life to enjoying dinner with Katrin at home after putting Moe to bed. Katrin glanced at me and winked. Katrin's wink at me means: it's going to be all right. To hell and back, I've taken a journey familiar to sufferers of Bipolar Disorder.

I agree to have Katrin come with me to all my psychiatric appointments and I promise to follow doctor's orders. We return to our life before I got pushed under the bus by depression. Unfortunately, Moe manifests a new aura of insecurity with me. He clings to Katrin when I leave to go to work or to run an errand. I take a month from work to be with him, hoping to allay his fears. I sense a subtle shift in my connection with my small son, feel guilty, and try to repair the rupture. My psychiatrist tells me I will know when Moe trusts me again and when Moe starts misbehaving again, my shrink tells me his trust is back. Katrin, Moe and I have a special party at the park to celebrate.

Moe's birthdays were a big deal and turned into extravaganzas when my mood was elevated. Katrin took over when my mood was low. The city offered thousands of venues for exciting children's birthday parties. Moe loved the attention and adored getting presents. For several years, his pre-school friends came, and then his elementary school friends, and then his high-school friends were added. Moe had lots of friends. He was the kid with two mothers. He was proud of his gay parents and had no hesitation to tell anyone and everyone.

Every summer, Katrin, Moe and I would go to England to visit Katrin's family, a very happy vacation with lots of celebrating. Katrin's sister had two kids with a boy a year younger than Moe and a girl two years younger. From England, we would visit Europe, Asia, South America and Africa. If Moe wasn't up to travel with us, he would stay with Katrin's family. Katrin's parents were divorced and remarried, providing four grandparents for Moe in England. They all lived near London and gathered together regularly. Katrin had been missed when she moved to New York. Occasionally, Katrin's relatives would visit us in New York and we would paint the town. Katrin's nephew and niece spent a summer with us when they were in high school.

Moe finished high school and went off to college in Boston before we were ready for him to go. I cried on and off for a month after he left. I missed him every day. He kept in close touch with Katrin and me. We visited back and forth when we could and we always managed a few weeks on Cape Cod or in the Hamptons during the summer. Moe took off to travel with his girlfriend, Jamie, after his senior year, before he started law school. Moe and Jamie married while Moe was still in law school. Jamie worked in public health. I never quite understand what she does exactly. Jamie is a jewel, level-headed, kind, smart, understanding and a welcome addition to the family. Amy and Maddy, their daughters came along and blew me away, Katrin too. Our granddaughters are the greatest!

4 MOE'S STORY

"Fucking Moe! Why is he doing this? What is going on with him? He was okay until the day he told me he was leaving. Fucking, fucking Moe!"

Tucked deep under the covers with my angry thoughts, I'm interrupted by Amy and Maddy jumping on top of me.

"Mommy, Mommy, we're hungry. Get up, we're hungry!"

I poke my head out blinking in the morning light. It's later than I think. The girls are ready for action and I'm a depressed lump under the covers. The girls refuse to cuddle in bed, pulling the covers down to my feet and tickling me. The dog gets into the act, licking my face. I put my dark thoughts on hold and pull myself out of bed. I throw on sweats and head downstairs to feed the kids and the dog.

"Is Daddy coming today?" Amy asked.

"Daddy is not coming today. He's at a workshop. He'll be here to pick you up tomorrow morning."

"What's a workshop?" Maddy asked.

"Where people work, silly," Amy said.

"Daddy's workshop is people doing art to feel better," I said.

"Is Daddy sick?" from Maddy.

I'm thinking 'Daddy is very, very sick,' but say, "No, Daddy is not sick. He wants to do artwork with people who can tell him how art can help him solve his problems."

"What problems?" from Amy.

"Why he moved out? Maddy asked.

"Kind of like that, you'll have to ask Daddy. He can tell you about his art therapy workshop."

"He doesn't tell you everything like he did before, does he?" Amy asked.

"That's right. Daddy and I are separated so we don't talk as much as before but we talk to plan to take the best care of you," I said, giving them hugs.

"What are we doing today?" Amy asked.

"How about we go to the park and ride bikes?"

"Then the café for treats?" Amy said.

"Bike riding and the café for treats, Maddy?"

"Yes, yes!"

Breakfast done, we head for the park and roll around the bike paths for hours with breaks to rest, to drink water and to plan our next route. Amy and Maddy like to devise dramas to add excitement to our ride. Memories of our bike rides with Moe haunt me and tears blur my vision of the world. Moe would develop exciting plots for us. We miss our creative director. Life without Moe is dull and drab. At the café, the girls start bickering about minor matters due to their fatigue and their continued adjustment to the separation.

"Amy, Maddy! I'm placing our order. Let's each pick out a treat! I'm going to have an oatmeal raisin cookie."

"I want a blueberry muffin," Amy said.

"Blueberry muffin, too," Maddy said.

"Good, very good."

Back at home, we have quiet time and then a spaghetti dinner, a favorite of the girls. After our showers and donning our pajamas, we cuddle on the sofa, watching a movie. When I tuck the girls into bed, Maddy wants to see Moe.

"Daddy's going to come tomorrow morning, honey. Go to sleep and when you wake up, it will be time to see Daddy.'

I sit with the girls as they drift off to sleep. As I crawl into a ball in my own bed, the telephone rings. I reach for the phone, pulling it under the covers and croak a greeting.

"Jamie, it's Moe. Are you all right? You sound funny."

"I'm in bed. Went bike-riding with the girls. Tired."

"Want me to come over for awhile?"

"No, I want you to move back in and be my husband again."

"Jamie, I'm sorry."

"I know, I know, you have to find out who you are. How's that working?"

"Jamie, I'm sorry you have to go through this."

"How did your workshop go today?"

"If crying a lot is good, it was good. If crying a lot is bad, it was bad. I guess only time will tell if it was useful. My therapist thought it might help."

"What were you crying about?"

"After we doodled around with the art materials, it was suggested we do a self-portrait. I already felt uncomfortable using art materials because Em was always pushing them on me relentlessly. I worked through my resistance and got going on my self-portrait."

"That was good."

"Yeah, the process was fun until I was driven by an urge to draw myself with a gash from my forehead, down my face and across my neck with bright red."

"Yikes!"

"The art therapist picked up on my distress and suggested I continue to use red. I covered my whole self-portrait with red and started to cry. The therapist sat with me while I cried and suggested I give my self-portrait a title."

"Did you?"

"I titled it, 'Moe-Moe'."

"And?"

"The therapist suggested I do another self-portrait. I worked long and hard and ended up with my head, neck and shoulders divided into small fragments with mini-scenes in each fragment. The scenes were from my past. It was overwhelming. I brought it back to the apartment. I dropped some tears doing that one but not like the bloody mess I made with the first one."

"Moe, sounds like you did some hard work."

"I think so too."

"The girls are looking forward to seeing you tomorrow."

"I'm looking forward to seeing them. I'll be there bright and early. Good night, Jamie!"

"Good night, Moe!"

Although exhausted, I could not fall asleep. Once again, I reviewed the events of the last six months. On December twenty-second, Moe received an urgent call from Katrin. When he returned her call, she told him that his mother had committed suicide. He got the next flight he could to New York. At Katrin and Emily's apartment, he read his mother's suicide note.

"Dear Moe, please forgive me. I just can't fight anymore. Even with meds, I cannot lift out of this excruciating darkness. The voices telling me to kill myself have won. Beyond my bipolar curse in the pure light, I love you, Jamie, Amy and Maddy. Do not blame yourself for you have been the light of my life. The pain has crushed me and I must extinguish myself to be free. Mom."

Emily had stayed at home for a month unable to work due to her bout of depression. Katrin and Moe had become inured to her downward spirals and expected her to recover with treatment as she always had in the past. Her psychiatrist had started another antidepressant and had mentioned electroconvulsive treatment if the pills were ineffective. Emily had kept her plans to commit suicide to herself. She always did because she didn't want to have to be hospitalized. Emily's mother, Annie, had died nine months before from cancer. The grief from the loss of her mother had eroded Emily's will to live. Katrin had been encouraged because Emily seemed to be in a better mood the day before she killed herself. Katrin had found Emily submerged and unconscious in the bathtub upon arriving home from work. EMS workers rushed her to the ER but she was dead on arrival. The autopsy revealed death was caused by a massive overdose of alcohol and pills.

Emily's death and memorial brought the public and the media out in force. Moe had a melt-down. He told me he didn't deserve to be loved, believing he had let his mother die. He stopped his life and jumped off into his own personal abyss. The bipolar burn had flared leaving him wounded and weak. He took an exit bow from my life. He rented a studio apartment, moved in and sank deep. Watching my life crack down the middle, I understood why Bipolar Disorder is called a 'family illness'. I wrongly believed that my little family had been spared but my husband and the father of my children has been crushed by the illness. Moe, the girls and I are keeping the psychotherapists of Boston in business now. As I drift off to sleep, I'm revisiting the boat ride off Long Island with Katrin and Moe, scattering Emily's ashes.

Moe's continued his retreat from life wracked with grief and guilt. Emily's suicide has taken him down. With her death by her own hand, he considers his life no longer worth living. His mother had left him many times before but she had always returned. With her final departure, he felt he could not go on. Months of therapy and medication helped quell his crazy thinking. He is starting to look forward to a time without Em's shadow haunting him.

Moe's sudden change following his mother's death smashed my belief in an orderly life. Moe explained to me he had grown up blown by winds of unpredictability which had resulted in his winding himself as tight as he could and keeping himself on one path without deviation. Em's death had unwound him leaving him without ground to stand on. With his psychologist's help, he put his pieces together. I appreciated Moe's openness and willingness to share his process with me. Moe is coming to terms with his mother's Bipolar Disorder and her suicide. Emily had experienced extended periods of joy, contentment, creativity, achievement and success. She met her challenges with determination and fortitude. Her suicide was tragic but a risk for people suffering from a major mental illness. Moe has been coming closer to accepting Emily's suicide in the context of her illness. He has friends and colleagues whose parents have died from heart disease and cancer. His mother has succumbed to Bipolar Disorder. Moe joined a group sponsored by a chapter of the National Alliance for the Mentally Ill. Gaining knowledge and support from the group proved invaluable to his wounded psyche. Attending the group lessened his sense of isolation, normalized his feelings and gave him support to address his loss. Moe makes a regular donation to NAMI in Emily's memory.

Moe has been considering leaving his law firm and running Em's business in New York. Katrin and Moe have started hypothetical rambles through the possibilities of Moe's continuing Em's fashion house. Both Katrin and Moe want to keep Em's name alive in the house she created, ensuring the continuity of Em's fashions. Em chose her employees wisely and guided them in her aesthetic vision. Katrin and Moe are steeped in Em's empire and ready to take over as a team.

Moe and I had a long discussion about getting back together and moving to New York. The challenges are daunting but I never stopped loving Moe. He took himself away from me and the girls to better put himself together after he fell apart with grief. He's worked hard to lift himself from despair and he's come back to me, Amy and Maddy. The girls are overjoyed to have their Daddy move home. Their many questions and concerns are being tactfully addressed. Over time, their trust will be restored. Their love has never wavered.

I am overjoyed to have him back and quickly agree to move to New York to support his venture with his mother's business. Moe had resisted his mother's attempts to pull him into her business and to make fashion his career. Now he wants to be part of her legacy.

"If my grief is driving me to carry on Em's work, I'll do it because no other doors are opening for me now. Taking the helm of Em's creation might pick me out of the water," Moe told me.

"Moe, you can't lose. Em's business is thriving. Having her son run the show will bring positive publicity and ease investor's and customer's fears with Em gone. Family fashion houses are the tradition."

"Katrin is pleased to keep the business in the family and I am relieved to make a change. I'm ready. What about you, Jamie?"

"Moe, I think the move will be good. I want to support you in any way I can. Amy and Maddy will adapt with our help. I work for the feds and can get a job transfer. It's going to be smooth. Let's research the best place to live, right away!"

"Let's tell Amy and Maddy."

"That's a great suggestion. Let me talk to Katrin, finalize the arrangement and we'll tell them together."

Moe paused and looked at me with a familiar look.

"Yes, Moe…"

Moe and I were back on track together, preparing ourselves for the big move to New York. We were in a better place together having weathered the loss of Emily and Moe's recovery from his intense grief. Moe and I arranged fun outings with the girls and talked about the impending move.

They both had questions and were relieved to have them answered. We visited Katrin in New York and made house-hunting an adventure for Amy and Maddy. Their input was invaluable as we toured the New York Metropolitan area until we found the perfect place. We all agreed on an apartment on the upper eastside within walking distance of Katrin's place. We shared our moments of missing Grandma Em as they arose. We would stop, talk and move on. Having the adventure of moving, helped us all move on.

We made the move and Moe threw himself into orbit at Em's fashion house. Moe's mood improved beyond his expectations. The learning curve had been steep as Moe wanted to know the business from the bottom up. He was a quick study and quickly assumed leadership of the company. Moe and Katrin had a relaxed working relationship. Katrin agreed to Moe's proposals and offered valuable advice. Katrin told Moe that she wanted him to take the lead as he would be running the business when she retired. Amy, Maddy and I visited Moe at Em's frequently. The girls loved the visits. Accustomed to long hours at the law firm, Moe was surprised to find his work finished at Em's at a reasonable time allowing him to spend more time with me and the girls. I liked having him home.

Moe wakes me up with a big smile. We wake the girls, have breakfast and head downtown.

"Why are we getting up so early on Saturday?" Amy asked.

"We are going to the NAMI march."

"What's the NAMI march?" Maddy asked.

"You know, Maddy, it's where people march in the streets to help people with mental illness," Amy answered.

"What's NAMI?" asked Maddy.

"You know, Maddy, right Dad? What's NAMI?" Amy said.

"NAMI stands for the National Alliance for the Mentally Ill. NAMI helps people with mental illness and the families of people with mental illness."

"What's mental illness?" Maddy asked.

"You know, Maddy, it's when people have trouble thinking and feeling and they need help to think and feel without any problems," Amy said.

"Good answer, Amy! Grandma Em had trouble with thinking and feeling and she needed help. NAMI helped me, too. NAMI helps people know about mental illness and helps to raise money to help people with mental illness. We're marching with people today to help, too," Moe said.

"Here we are!"

Moe, Jamie, Amy and Maddy join a group of people at the annual NAMI march. Everyone has been generously sponsored and the announcement of the large sum raised is greeted with rousing cheers and applause. We join hands behind the NAMI banner and start to march with thousands of people through the streets.

I squeeze Moe's hand and look into his eyes.

"You all right, Moe?"

"Never better."

ABOUT THE AUTHOR

Carol Neves has worked as a Mental Health Clinician and an art therapist. She is an advocate for community mental health services. She has a Masters degree in Clinical Counseling and Family Psychology.

www.ingramcontent.com/pod-product-compliance
Lightning Source LLC
Chambersburg PA
CBHW072338290526
45794CB00002B/931